Unsettled Matters

Unsettled Matters

The Life and Death of BRUCE LEE

A Biography by

TOM BLEECKER

Originally published by
Gilderoy Publications / Lompoc, California

Now published by
McLisa Publications / Shawne, Kansas

UNSETTLED MATTERS

First edition published 1996
Gilderoy Publications, Lompoc, California
Printed in the United States of America

Second edition published 2002
Rising Sun Productions
Printed in Canada
Revised layout by Tosha Lord Graphics

01 00 99 98 97 96 5 4 3 2 1

Library of Congress Catalog Card Number 96-94563

ISBN (paperback): 0-9653132-0-4

Parts of Chapter 20 of the present work appeared in an issue of Karate Illustrated magazine (Vol.3 #6) January 1993

With all our most holy illusions knocked
higher than Gilderoy's kite,

We have had a jolly good lesson, and serves
us
jolly well right!

~ Kipling

About The Author

In August 1973 while his body was being flown from Hong Kong to Seattle, Washington, Bruce Lee's coffin mysteriously opened and the dye from his dark blue suit bled onto the coffin's white silk interior. The ancient Chinese saw it as a bad omen. "The buried man will not live in peace!" they proclaimed, "There are unsettled matters!"

Considered one of the foremost authorities on Bruce Lee today, Tom Bleecker not only trained privately with Lee, but the two shared numerous mutual friends in the martial arts community as well as the Hollywood film industry. Moreover, Bleecker co-authored with Bruce's widow, Linda Lee, The Bruce Lee Story, which served as the source material for MCA Universal's motion picture Dragon.

Unsettled Matters is the result of over four years of intense investigative research that led the author from the back alleys of Hong Kong to obscure court documents uncovered in Los Angeles and Seattle. Learn the truth about the life and death of martial arts icon Bruce Lee. Discover why both the author and the first publication company had been threatened with massive civil lawsuits if they dare publish the contents of this book.

The Author, Tom Bleecker

CONTENTS

Part One

The Life of Bruce Lee

Introduction

It was a cold, rainy night thirty-nine years ago in Los Angeles, and Ed Parker's black belt class had just ended. I sat in the dressing room gazing at my right shin. There was a swollen lump the size of a golf ball, and the pain was excruciating. I took off my sweat-drenched karate uniform and noted fresh blood on the sleeve of the recently torn rice cloth. I looked for cuts but couldn't find any. Someone else's blood. Ed Parker ran a tough class because Ed Parker was tough. Real tough. Street tough. Hawaiian-born, six-feet tall and a solid 220 pounds, and thought by many to be as fast and as powerful as Muhammad Ali.

The student roster of the advanced class read like "The Wild Bunch." We had a couple of ex-felons, several Hell's Angels, a recent Mr. Universe, and a college football hero, among others.

On the tournament circuit there was a group of Parker's students who became known as "The Wrecking Crew." And they fought anyone and everyone. Their most formidable foe was a nearby Tang Soo Do school, whose head instructor was a young man named Chuck Norris.

Ed Parker's most notorious black belt hung out in Memphis. His name was Elvis Presley, and he didn't own a guitar upon which our school emblem wasn't prominently displayed. It was a select group of Ed Parker's black belts who later became known as the infamous Memphis Mafia. Men whose sole purpose was to protect "The King."

Back in the sixties when the martial art was in its infancy in this country, it was amazing what power the lay public bestowed upon the elite few who wore the black belts. Mysterious, intimidating, at times even cryptic, many of these men were revered as superhumans, if not gods. If there was a spiritual aspect to this eastern philosophy of deadly fighting, it eluded us Westerners in the worst way. For the most part, we have always been a brawn society, evidenced in the early 1960s as we oiled our vast war machinery for transport to the jungles of Vietnam.

I carried my shoes and walked across the mats barefoot, noting a new hole in the plaster wall where Bob Cook had kicked Larry Hartsell dangerously close to the plate glass mirrors. I was sitting in the small waiting room putting on my shoes when Ed Parker suddenly emerged from his office and headed for the back of the school.

Two Chinese men entered through the rear door and were greeted by Parker. The shorter, more reserved, of the two men was James Lee. James had often driven from Oakland to visit Parker, and this time brought with him an unknown kung-fu practitioner from Hong Kong, who was meeting Parker for the first time. His name was Bruce Lee. He was a well dressed, good looking man in his mid-twenties. In sharp contrast to Parker, Bruce stood a mere five-feet-seven inches and weighed around 140 pounds.

Soon Parker and Bruce began to exchange ideas, with Bruce often using James Lee (no relation to Bruce) to demonstrate his point. Above all else, what instantly impressed me about Bruce was his unmistakable self-confidence. In the two years since

I had begun training with Ed Parker, Bruce Lee was the first man who did not appear intimidated by this massive Hawaiian. Although this meeting took place almost forty years ago, three distinct characteristics still stand out in my mind: the intense level of enthusiasm with which Bruce expressed his art; his awesome physical and emotional energy; and most notably the incredible speed of his hands.

Over the next six years Bruce and I spent a great deal of time in each other's company. In addition to training together in the martial arts, we had both become involved in the Hollywood film industry and, as a result, shared a common life-style and numerous mutual friends.

The day Bruce died in Hong Kong on July 20, 1973 I was having lunch with Blake Edwards and Julie Andrews. Like so many others, I had either known firsthand or heard secondhand about Bruce's troubles, his extreme weight loss, his life-threatening hospitalization nine weeks earlier, his violent and unpredictable mood swings, his deep depression and growing paranoia, his drinking and drug use, his alleged womanizing, his ongoing battle with the press and his seemingly endless list of enemies. And now he was dead. Dead at the age of thirty-two, curiously from brain edema. In lay-terms his brain simply swelled up inside his head. The problem was the doctors had no idea why.

Fifteen years later I produced a tribute to martial arts Grandmaster Edmund Parker, which was held at the Bonaventure Hotel in Los Angeles on February 27, 1988. Over a thousand friends, students and martial arts dignitaries sat down to a five-course dinner and were entertained throughout the evening. In addition, scores of television and film celebrities came from all over the world to pay tribute to Ed Parker, along with his entire immediate family, many of whom were flown in from Hawaii and Utah. It was truly a grand evening held on a grand scale. Although Ed, at age fifty-seven, was thirty pounds overweight and was occasionally bothered with gout, the martial arts community was stunned when he two years later died in a Honolulu airport of a massive heart attack.

In the early planning stage of the tribute, I wrote a letter to Bruce Lee's widow, Linda, inviting her to attend on behalf of Bruce. I had not seen Linda since Bruce's death, and I was pleased when I learned that she had accepted my invitation.

On the evening of the tribute, Linda was accompanied by a man named Adrian Marshall. Back in the mid-sixties, Marshall had trained for a brief period at Parker's WLA school. Later he became Bruce Lee's attorney. Although he had been married for over thirty-five years, Marshall often escorted Linda to various functions having to do with Bruce.

The following week, Linda and I talked on the telephone, specifically in regard to a book she had been commissioned to write for Ohara Publications. Essentially it was to be an authorized biography of Bruce Lee. She had a problem, however. Although she'd been advanced a considerable sum of money to write the book, she couldn't get beyond the first page.

In addition to having been for years a close personal friend and student of Bruce's, over the past twenty years I had worked as a professional screenwriter, and so I was a prime candidate to help Linda out of her dilemma. Shortly after our conversation, I traveled to Linda's home in Los Angeles, where she and I discussed the prospect and finally agreed to work together.

The book that Linda had proposed was actually a

rewrite of a Dell paperback first published in 1975. The book was called Bruce Lee: The Man Only I Knew, which had been ghost-written by an English writer named Alan Shadrake, with Linda being listed as author. At the time Linda and I co-authored The Bruce Lee Story (Ohara Publications), Linda was employed as a kindergarten teacher in Torrance and, as a result, I often worked alone.

On the day that I began my research, Linda had left a copy of Shadrake's book in a large room adjacent to the garage. Essentially, everything having to do with Bruce was located in that room, primarily in six large filing cabinets and two closets which, collectively, I was to use as my research material. As to an office, we agreed that we would work in either that room or in Linda's office, which was located at the opposite end of the house.

The room that housed Bruce's files was the only secured room in the home, which I immediately discerned from the barred windows. Off to one side were Bruce's legendary six black journals, each of which was over five inches thick. Collectively these journals were written by Bruce during his well-publicized back injury in 1970 and allegedly contained the entire source material of Bruce's personal martial art of Jeet Kune Do. Several years after Bruce died, Linda had authorized the publication of The Tao of Jeet Kune Do, which purportedly contained the deep and highly secretive wisdom contained in these six journals. And here I stood looking at the actual journals. To a martial artist the experience was akin to a lay Christian stumbling upon the Dead Sea Scrolls.

A nearby closet door was open, and I flipped on the light and walked inside. Bruce's old boxing gloves, the leather now cracked and faded, were hanging on a wall.

Nearby, Bruce's protective headgear, a vast array of martial arts weaponry, a rusted set of weights, jump ropes and a tattered heavy bag. Along one wall were two army footlockers stuffed with unopened fan letters written to Linda after Bruce's death. Sprawled on the floor were the electric shock stimulator and its entanglement of wires and electrodes Bruce used to affix to his muscles so he could exercise even while he slept. I had heard about this electronic contraption, but I'd never seen it. It looked like it once belonged to the German Gestapo. The sight of it made me queasy, and I closed the door.

To this day I find it difficult to believe that Linda had not anticipated my troubled reaction to what I discovered in the filing cabinets she had directed me to. To begin with, there were far too many lawsuits and medical records. More startling was the voluminous merchandising deals which had been spearheaded by the marketing company Ziv International. How had all this merchandising become connected to the martial arts in Bruce's name? How and why had Bruce's beloved art of kung fu become tied to Madison Avenue? Had this been necessary for Linda and her two children to survive financially after Bruce's death? And what did Adrian Marshall, the man who had accompanied Linda to the tribute, have to do with this? Curiously, his name was attached to practically everything.

The majority of the cabinet space contained hundreds of legal files, which were housed in an orderly fashion, with the remaining, far less organized space devoted to everything else. In a lower drawer I discovered Bruce's old wallet, his driver's license and his money clip. Elsewhere, hundreds of files dealing with his final years in Hong Kong, including personal correspondences with Hong Kong producers

Raymond Chow and Run Run Shaw. Seemingly Linda had kept everything that had ever belonged to Bruce.

In another cabinet one file stood out among all the others: "BRUCE'S AUTOPSY REPORT." I sat down and read it. By the time I had finished reading it for the third time, I felt sick. Something was wrong. Not just with the autopsy report, but with everything.

At that moment I found myself thinking about Bruce's Hong Kong funeral and how his HK$40,000 (US$8,500) bronze coffin had mysteriously opened during transit to Seattle, and how moisture had entered and caused the dye from his dark blue suit to bleed onto the coffin's white silk interior. The ancient Chinese saw it as a bad omen. "The buried man will not live in peace," they proclaimed. "There are unsettled matters."

I retrieved Shadrake's book and turned for the door. As I reached for the light switch, I noticed a second closet. This one was closed. I hesitated for a moment and then opened it. It was filled with Bruce's old clothes. His ties, shirts and suits. Fifteen years had passed, and the master's clothes, now faded, hung limp on thin wire hangers. Along the wall was a dresser containing his socks and underwear, along with half-used bottles of after-shave lotion. All this had been brought back from Hong Kong. I closed the door, turned off the light, and left the only room in the house with barred windows.

Walking to the opposite end of the house, I entered Linda's office. Although the rest of the home had a warm, friendly air, this particular room was dark and impersonal. I sat in the worn leather chair that was situated behind Bruce's old desk and directly across from an open closet where Bruce's five hundred pound safe sat on the floor.

I read through Shadrake's book and found it difficult, if not impossible, to concentrate. There was a thick film of dust on the top of the desk and several piles of unopened junk mail. I could hardly believe the postmark -- 1982! Six years was a long time for junk mail to be sitting on one's desk. What had happened six years earlier that seemingly resulted in Linda abandoning her office? My writer's mind was whirling, and it was then that I first began to wonder what I had got myself into.

I read Shadrake's book a second time, then placed it on the desk. Although the story was touching, it didn't gel with much of what I'd seen in the "Bruce Lee Room." I needed to make some notes. I opened the top drawer to Linda's desk in search of a pen, only to find myself staring down the personal stationary of Adrian Marshall. Resting atop the stationary was a beautiful plexiglas gavel with "Adrian Marshall" engraved across the handle. What was Adrian Marshall's stationary doing in Linda's desk? Was this Adrian's office? What would he be doing with an office in Linda's house. And why did it appear that no one had been in this room for six years?

Just then I heard a car pulling up outside and realized that Linda had arrived home from work. I walked back through the house and opened the front door to see her stepping out of Bruce's 1973 red 350SL Mercedes. Sixteen years had passed since Bruce's death, and she was still driving his car. I was happy to see her, although I must admit I had begun to feel a bit like the writer that William Holden played in the film classic Sunset Boulevard.

Over the next six weeks I researched the life and death of Bruce Lee from the cradle to the grave and then continued on through the next seven years during which

Bruce lived as the legal embodiment of "The Estate of Bruce Lee." The task was exhausting, and when I had finished, my co-author and I had a serious problem. Although I conceded to Linda that the basic story that served as the foundation of Shadrake's book was generally true, it was at the same time unmistakably incomplete, in several critical places grossly inaccurate, and altogether too frequently misleading. Paramount to all else, I strongly believed that Bruce's autopsy report, together with the coroner's inquest into his death, had been a whitewash.

A few months into the book project Adrian Marshall surfaced with a business deal he'd been working on. He was always working on something to promote the Lee legend. This time his sights were on MCA Universal, and it appeared that he had landed a feature film on the life of Bruce Lee. As fate would have it, the film (Dragon, subsequently released in 1993) was tied to the book Linda and I were currently writing. Regarding the contract, itself, there was one specific clause that threatened to squash the entire deal if MCA Universal refused to agree to it.

The clause, listed under contract limitations, read: "Company agrees that no publication or theatrical or television motion picture hereunder shall make any reference to (i) the use of marijuana by Bruce Lee or (ii) to sexual or romantic relationships between Bruce Lee and any woman other than his wife during the years of his marriage or (iii) to any unsavory or illicit circumstances surrounding his death." It was this last instruction to avoid specific elements of Bruce's demise that I found particularly disturbing.

During the writing of <u>The Bruce Lee Story</u>, at several junctures I thought about packing up my pencils and returning home. The reason I didn't is that I had fallen in love with Linda. Through all the trials and tribulations of our creative endeavor, the vulnerability and sheer emotional depth of this woman found their way into my heart. And so I was torn, and I think Linda was torn, too. On the one hand was this extremely troublesome biography about a man who was not only her former husband but had also been a close friend of mine, while on the other hand was this wonderful budding romance that was all too quickly sweeping us both off our feet.

Our serendipitous coming together had a true storybook ending, and Linda and I were married in the summer of 1988. Our honeymoon would be short-lived, however. Ostensibly the unsettled matters that the Chinese people had warned about inevitably took a death grip on our marriage and simply would not let go. Ultimately Linda and I could not resolve several devastating issues, and our brief marriage ended in divorce.

Over the years Linda has often stated publicly that she prefers to talk about how Bruce lived. I wholeheartedly agree with her. What follows is the book I would have preferred that Linda and I had co-authored seven years ago. I say this because I believe that Bruce, who spent his entire public life speaking out against false pretenses and defined Tao as "truth," would have wanted nothing less than a full and honest public accounting of his life.

And finally, as I ponder what lies ahead, I remember the story that Ed Parker told at the tribute. He was always the consummate storyteller, and he recalled the time when the teacher got before the class and said, "'If there is anyone in this classroom who's stupid, please stand.' No one did, and he repeated himself, 'If there's anyone in this room who's stupid, please stand!' and little Johnny stood up. And the teacher said, 'Little Johnny, are you stupid?' And Johnny replied, 'No, teacher, I'm not, but I just hated seeing you stand up there alone.'"

I hope I'm not the schoolteacher standing up there alone. Let us begin.

The author while doing research in Hong Kong.

Chapter 1

Hong Kong

It all began over several thousand kilos of opium seized by the Chinese from the hulls of British cargo ships and subsequently dumped into the Yellow Sea. The attempt by the British to establish a drug market in China had failed miserably. Within the hour the British opium dealers were dragged in chains to the frozen tundra of Central Asia, and one was even publicly crucified on the Canton docks.

The queen stiffened. Together with the king's ransom worth of opium fed to the crab population at the bottom of the ocean, this business of publicly lynching a British subject on the stinking docks was nothing less than barbaric, and the angry British responded by ruthlessly shelling the coastline.

When the dust settled, Britain's sole diplomat in China, Trade Superintendent Captain Charles Elliot, wanted more than a perfunctory apologetic tea with the emperor. Perhaps a piece of land would be in order, a token tidbit? A tiny uninhabited slice from the great vastness of China?

Within the hour Elliot had a handful of scribbled paperwork before the emperor, and in a nineteenth century exercise of gunboat diplomacy Hong Kong Island was handed over to the British.

The Crown's Trade Secretary, Lord Pomerson, soon apprised Her Majesty Queen Victoria of the Crown's newly acquired tropical paradise. This place, which he dismissed as a "barren island with hardly a house upon it," had few resources, typhoons were fierce and frequent, and its people were subject to malaria, cholera, typhoid and bubonic plague. Worst of all, the coastline was steep jagged rock, and there wasn't a single fresh water river anywhere in sight. The island did, however, have one redeeming quality. Hong Kong possessed a deep-water harbor that could serve as shelter from the frequent typhoons.

The Queen Elizabeth Hotel

As a trading post, Hong Kong could not compete with the rich mainland ports like Shanghai and for years served as a haunt for pirates, smugglers and other assorted malcontents of the British Empire. Besides a large population of criminals known as triads who had fled Communist China, Hong Kong's early administrations were fraught with scandalous characters – incompetents, exploiters, distressed judiciary, and corrupt police.

Like practically everyone else, the Japanese had been flexing their muscles at China for years. In the summer of 1940, the general opinion circulating in Hong Kong was that, as crazy as the Japanese were acting, they weren't crazy enough to attack this famous outpost of the British Crown.

Li Hoi Chuen, who was originally from the village of Futshan in Canton, fled Communist China with thousands of other Chinese who by hook or crook found their way to Hong Kong Island in the late 1930s. When Hoi Chuen wasn't performing with Hong Kong's Cantonese Opera, which was more a community theater group than a world renowned company like the Peking Opera and offered little pay, he could routinely be found in the local gambling halls and opium dens. In June 1940, he stood beside his attractive wife, Grace, who at the age of nineteen had come to the island from Shanghai, as together they watched the beaches being wired. Nearby, government buildings were being sandbagged against bomb blast. Soon Hong Kong's Chinese residents were practicing blackouts while European families were hurriedly being evacuated to the safety of Australia.

Prior to the passage of the Nationality Act of 1940, Chinese residing in the United States were disbarred from becoming citizens, either by birth or naturalization. This changed on October 11, 1940 when President Roosevelt signed the Nationality Act of 1940 into law. It was around this time frame that Hoi Chuen and Grace, together with the members of the Cantonese Opera, booked passage by ocean liner to the United States where the company opened in San Francisco. Shortly after their arrival, so the story goes, Grace was shocked to discover that she was eight months pregnant.

On November 27, 1940 Grace was wheeled into the Jackson Street Hospital in San Francisco's Chinatown. Hours later she gave birth to a baby boy (by law one of the first Chinese American citizens under the newly signed Nationality Act), whom she named Li Jun Fan. The nickname "Bruce" was given to the infant by a hospital worker.

Bruce's mother, Grace.

Sixty years ago the quality of medical service available to the common Chinese in Hong Kong and Communist China was relatively poor, and consequently many infants died in their first year. Having come to believe that these infants had been taken by gods who placed a much higher value on male children than on female offspring, it was a common practice amongst the Chinese to give their male infants female names in an attempt to fool the gods. It was for this reason the Li family (note: Lee is the Americanized spelling of Li), in addition to giving Bruce the names Li Yuen Kam and Li Sui Loong ("Little Dragon"), gave him a girl's nickname, Sai Fon ("Little Phoenix"), and had one of his ears pierced.

With their temporary visas nearing expiration, Hoi Chuen and his wife were forced to return to Hong Kong in early 1941. The place was pretty much as they had remembered it.

One of several misconceptions about Bruce Lee is that he came from a wealthy family. Often one will read the misleading phrase "by Hong Kong standards" in reference to the Li home, which was located in Kowloon above a row of crowded shops and was anything but a showpiece for Better Homes and Gardens. In addition to Bruce's parents and four siblings, 218 Nathan Road was bed and board to Bruce's aunt and her five children, as well as a servant couple and their son Wu Ngan, who decades later, as Lee's butler, would be targeted by the press as a prime suspect in Bruce Lee's mysterious death.

Beyond the accordion steel door were several sparsely furnished, partitioned areas. None of the nearly twenty occupants had his or her own bedroom, but instead, cramped sleeping areas had been sectioned off throughout the tiny dwelling. Although there was a bathroom, the tub was often used during periods of drought to hold water for cooking and flushing the toilet.

Apart from the thousands of Chinese who were living in crude shantytowns made of sticks, canvas, cardboard and corrugated iron, and thousands more who lived as elevated squatters on apartment building rooftops, the Li family lived like the vast majority of Chinese residing in Hong Kong in the spring of 1941, packed like sardines into dilapidated apartment dwellings and surrounded by an urban bee hive of garish neon signs and clamorous shop fronts. Amid the smells of spice, incense, wok oil, open sewer systems, perfume and body sweat, the blaring of radio music, the ceaseless clatter of spoons, Mahjongg tiles, coins, abaci, hammers and electric drills, Bruce suffered miserably that summer at the hand of the sweltering heat and humidity that engulfed Hong Kong Island and neighboring Kowloon.

Another misconception about Bruce Lee is that he was born into this world with rippling muscles and boundless energy. To the contrary, Bruce was an extremely fragile child from the beginning and was abnormally slow in his physical development. The reason was that he was born with a medical condition known as cryptorchidism, which is a disorder wherein one or both of the newborn's testicles have failed to descend prior to birth. The condition is often routinely corrected by the administration of androgen hormone, which the infant and its mother failed to produce in the infant's eighth fetal month. Although it is not known if Bruce was treated for this abnormality in his early childhood, what is a matter of medical record is that the primary defect remained uncorrected in Bruce until well into his adult years.

As a result of Bruce's cryptorchidism, Bruce's bone and muscle growth were impeded, and during his lifetime his reproductive system never developed beyond adolescence. As to the well-developed and highly defined muscular body that earned him the title of "the fittest man in the world," regardless of his much-publicized physical workouts, this Herculean physique was simply not a natural genetic possibility. Moreover, vitally important to understanding Bruce's early years is the knowledge that a primary symptom seen in most children with untreated cryp torchidism is psychosocial immaturity.

On December 8, 1941 the Japanese crossed the border into Hong Kong. The following night the 38th Division of the Japanese Army attacked with grenades and machine guns an area just north of Kowloon known as Smuggler's Ridge, simultaneously bombing and shelling nearby Kai Tak Airport, blowing the Royal Air Force to bits. By daybreak Japanese gunners were shelling across the harbor while dive-bombers screamed down on Central, and for the first time in history utter chaos struck the waterfront.

Hong Kong fell quickly to the Japanese on Christmas day 1941, after a token, but desperate fight by Hong Kong volunteers, British and Indian Army regulars, and a raw untested expeditionary unit from Canada. In nearby Kowloon, Bruce's father, Hoi Chuen, had narrowly escaped death when a bomb crashed through the roof of the opium den he was patronizing. Although the bomb never exploded, it crushed to death the man sleeping dreamily on the neighboring cot.

Within a few weeks Japan's military governor Lieutenant-General Rensuke Isogai posted his first proclamation on the pedestal of Queen Victoria's statue in Statue Square: "For those who transgress the path of right and do not keep within their correct places, I will deal with these according to military law, without mercy."

The conduct of the Japanese in Hong Kong was deplorable. Immediately after the surrender they deliberately let their troops run wild, raping and looting everywhere. While the Kempeitai (the military police) tortured prisoners as readily and as brutally as the Gestapo, the Chinese population at large was treated with blatant arrogance. Passersby who failed to bow to Japanese soldiers were slapped on the face or hit with a rifle butt. Many others were unceremoniously jailed. As the legend goes, it was during this time that Bruce, barely out of diapers, is alleged to have stood on apartment rooftops, angrily shaking his fist at Japanese planes flying overhead.

The Japanese occupation presented the large population of Hong Kong triads with an unparalleled opportunity to solidify control over the black market and the vice trades. With the elimination of the British administration and police, triad syndicates reached agreement with the Japanese and were allowed to run the colony's illegal business in return for providing the Japanese with intelligence information and helping them maintain order. Also, as part of their agreement, the Japanese destroyed the Hong Kong police records on triads.

As a mere youngster, Bruce watched his homeland deteriorate. The schools literally emptied. Food and fuel became desperately short, and everywhere there were street gangs run by organized criminals who virtually dictated which Chinese would eat and which would go hungry. With the police barely able to keep up with the daily volume of serious crime, much less focus on the major syndicates, the triads used the police problems to their benefit. During the large postwar police recruitment drive, hundreds of triad members secretly joined the Japanese police force.

Then in August 1945, following an Americana atom bomb dropped on Hiroshima, Sir Cecil Harcourt of the royal Navy steamed into "Fragrant Harbor" at the head of the British fleet to reestablish Her Majesty's presence in the war-ravaged British Crown Colony of Hong Kong. Although the Chinese were relieved to see the British reclaim Government House, the relationship between the

Dragon and the Lion continued to be mutually dispassionate. Chinese were still of the Middle Kingdom and to them everyone else was a barbarian. Though they feigned a docile submission, the Chinese merely tolerated the British. When Bruce was a child, theaters used to blare "God Save the Queen" as a closing finale, but the practice was dropped because of the lack of patriotic reaction. A few British would stand staunchly throughout the anthem while the Chinese audience shuffled out indifferently. Slow to change, nearly two decades later in 1964, Hong Kong made history by being the only city in the world in which Britain's famed mopheads—the Beatles—lost money.

Beginning at age six and continuing to age eighteen, Bruce frequently worked in Mandarin films, in which he appeared in over two dozen productions. To label him a child star, however, as if he were the Far East counterpart to Mickey Rooney, would be grossly misleading. The Mandarin film industry has never had child stars as we know them in the western world. What they have are children who appear in Mandarin films.

It is true that Bruce was a poor student in school and, other than average marks in art and history, received failing grades and was frequently suspended for acting up in class and fighting. Not unlike its business world, even as far back as the 1950s Hong Kong's education system was fiercely competitive, so much so that a child's future was dictated by his kindergarten credentials.

As a troubled and uncentered child, at the age of fifteen Bruce took an avid interest in the martial arts. As a footnote, during that time in Hong Kong most martial arts schools were either triad societies per se or had triad affiliations.

Initially Bruce had been exposed to the graceful movement of tai chi, but he quickly became bored with what he perceived as ineffectiveness and began studying the Hung style of kung fu. Eventually he left the Hung style as well, allegedly because he had been defeated in a fight. In reality, from the beginning and up to the day of his death, Bruce was only interested in a martial arts system that would teach him to be victorious in the street.

Bruce had for some time been attracted to the Wing Chun style of kung fu because its students rarely lost street fights. In 1956 when Bruce joined the Wing Chun school, the style was taught by Grandmaster Yip Man, who was a good friend of Bruce's father Hoi Chuen, the two having first met as natives of a small village in Canton. Legendary in his own right, Yip Man, who weighed less than 110 pounds, was, according to Bruce, the hardest puncher he had ever met and purportedly had killed a man with a single punch.

In the initial learning phases the going was rough, and Bruce was frequently knocked down in class. By the end of his first year, however, he had become one of Yip Man's most promising students and soon became obsessed with one day being top gun. By the end of his second year, he had advanced to the level of an intermediate student, who frequently and defiantly pounded his fists on his chest. His brother Robert recalled, "Bruce was the king gorilla, boss of the whole school (Bruce's high school)." And even Yip Man had reflected that "Bruce was completely absorbed and was fighting crazy."

It is well known that as a young adult Bruce had a strong allegiance to street gangs and could often be found roaming the streets with chains and knives. It is also true that triads have always used these streetwise thugs as temporary muscle. In sharp contrast to the youth gangs well known in the United States, Hong Kong gang members have always maintained a clean-cut appearance and kept their hair short. As to the higher echelon of triad officers, they are in sharp contrast to the Mafia chieftains paraded before television cameras in the U.S. Dressed in dark blue and gray suits and conservative shirts and ties, they look more like bankers than godfathers.

Historically no one has ever confirmed that Bruce Lee ever officially joined a particular triad. Perhaps this is because admitted triad membership has always been a serious crime in Hong Kong. Moreover, triad members take a sworn blood oath of secrecy. With rare exception, triad members would rather die than violate this oath, even when dragged before the United States Senate Subcommittee on Organized Crime.

In the late 1970s, however, a notorious triad kingpin sentenced to a U.S. prison talked off the record. His name was simply Ma. "When I was fourteen years old, I joined the triad. Just like the organizations that everybody joins, one must take an oath to sworn secrecy, promising never to reveal anything about the triad organization. My joining the triad was a very natural process because when I was ten years old, I had been hanging out with triad members and played with them. Since I was rather young, not very much was requested of me, but in a few years time I joined in the street fights in order to protect our turf. We often fought with the Sun Yee On and the Wo Shing Wo triads. When I was eighteen, while still a triad member I took an exam and joined the Royal Hong Kong Police."

Tantamount to all else, what is etched in stone in the

form of a triad blood oath is that membership in a triad is for life. There is no way around this. A made member is owned by the triad kingpins until death.

As Bruce entered his teenage years, life in the colony began to worsen. In March 1952 riots broke out in Kowloon when the government refused to allow a mission from Canton to aid victims of a squatter fire. Then in 1953 on Christmas Day, Hong Kong's Shek Kip Mei squatter area burst into flames leaving 53,000 people homeless, this to be followed in 1956 with another human floodtide of immigrants. With Hong Kong's population soaring over the 2.5 million mark, squatter huts began appearing in every available crevice. With the onset of the summer's heat and humidity, rioting and bloodshed between Nationalists and Communists exploded in the streets.

Though they were banned, restricted and distrusted by most countries in the world, especially by their Asian neighbors, Hong Kong's Chinese population faced a grim austerity not unlike that from which most had fled. For many young men the only solution was to throw in their hands and withdraw into the dream world of opium or undertake a life of street crime. Back in the late 1950s, Bruce Lee's prospects weren't much better. There was no money to be made in the martial arts, and as far as pursuing an acting career in Mandarin films or excelling in education, the outlook was even more dismal.

Fact: In Hong Kong a man's self-worth is directly proportional to his ability to make money. To understand the driving force that propelled Bruce Lee from the cradle to the grave, it is imperative that one heavily underscores the supreme value he placed on the acquisition of the almighty dollar. The reason is simple. Hong Kong has always been a city where money is god. Throughout Hong Kong gaudy signs of success have always been plentiful—pink Rolls Royces and pink mink coats, jewel-encrusted gold watches, private nightclubs that charge businessmen $1,500 just to sit with a hostess for several hours, personalized license plates with lucky numbers that cost car owners up to $175,000, the world's most expensive office building cast in marble and glass at a cost of $1 billion. Hong Kong is a city where a handful of mega-rich Chinese move from one social excess to another. Above all else, Hong Kong has always been a place where business takes precedence over every other human pursuit, where success is measured by the number of cars, furs, Oriental antiques and diamonds one owns, and by the height at which one lives on "The Peak." How one obtains his money is of little importance to the people of Hong Kong. The fact that he has it is all that has ever mattered.

Fact number two, which has never changed: In Hong Kong only the rich immigrate. To fully discern the total picture of Bruce's childhood years in Hong Kong, one cannot ignore the fact that he was born in San Francisco and, consequently, was legally an American citizen by birthright.

To be a Chinese-American citizen living in Hong Kong in the 1940-50s made Bruce Lee worth his weight in diamonds. In the final analysis he didn't need school, and he didn't have to sidle up to anyone, be they family, friend, or foe. Like the Prodigal Son, all he had to do was return to the place of his birth and claim his inheritance. Understandably this rare title, this semblance to European royalty, contributed to Bruce's cocksuredness because it made him a big man in many circles and with many Chinese, for with his eventual passage to the United States, others could follow in his wake, either by marriage or sponsorship, which several family members later did.

By the mid-1950s triad crime was completely out of control, and the Hong Kong police commissioner, under strong pressure from London, organized the Triad Society Bureau. Almost overnight the British administration launched its first earnest war against the triads, arresting more than 10,000 triad members. Many were imprisoned, other deported, while the majority entered a system of police supervision similar to probation.

In the fall of 1958, with the approach of Bruce's eighteenth birthday, Grace sat down with Bruce and other members of the family. Bruce's older brother Peter spoke candidly about what he had heard on the street. Bruce had made many enemies. Some of them were triads who had openly talked about killing Bruce. At the young age of seventeen, Bruce had already set himself on a collision course and was destined to become crab bait at the bottom of the polluted Hong Kong harbor. It was time for Bruce Lee to get out of Hong Kong.

As a matter of policy, before a Chinese citizen was allowed to leave Hong Kong Island for the United States, the individual had to obtain from the police department a certificate clearing them of any police criminal record. When Bruce applied for this certificate, the police informed him that he was on a known gangster list. It took considerable doings to clear Bruce's name before his departure.

With the Grim Reaper approaching, it was finally time for the Prodigal Son to return home to claim his long-awaited inheritance. And so on October 14, 1958 Bruce Lee boarded the third class section of the American President's Line with a single folded $100 bill in his shirt pocket and, promising his father he would "make his fortune," sailed back to the city of his birth, having decided he would become a dentist.

Chapter 2

The Seattle Years

Following the eighteen-day passage across the Pacific, the ship docked in San Francisco, returning Bruce Lee to the city of his birth. For several months Bruce hung around San Francisco's Chinatown teaching dance, but his stay was short-lived, owing to a problem involving someone or some group of individuals in the Chinese community. There is little known about this matter, only that there was a problem.

What is known is that around this time Bruce's mother called a friend of the family who lived in Seattle, a highly influential Chinese woman named Ruby Chow, and that Bruce quickly left the Bay area. Ping Chow, a fellow member of the Cantonese Opera and close friend of Bruce's father, had been nursed back to health in New York by Ruby when the company had been stranded in the states with the outbreak of World War II. Years later, following her marriage to Ping, Ruby had been elected a county commissioner in Seattle.

Bruce Lee faced a tough customer in Ruby Chow, who owned a three-story building that was both home and workplace for many young Chinese immigrants pursuing a new life in America. The ground floor housed the first Chinese restaurant established outside the borders of Seattle's Chinatown, and the upper two floors served as living quarters.

Upon his arrival from San Francisco, Bruce moved into a tiny bedroom on the third floor of Ruby Chow's. During the day he attended Edison Tech High School, and in the evening he worked in the restaurant bussing tables. Soon her took a second, early morning job, stuffing newspapers at The Seattle Times.

Outside of Ruby Chow's

Around this time Bruce met a man who became his first student and assistant instructor in the United States, a sensitive and intelligent man named Jesse Glover. In his book Bruce Lee, Glover recalled spending the first six months working with Bruce on some adjustment problems his friend and teacher was having.

According to Glover, although in Hong Kong Bruce had reveled in his prominent street status, in America he was viewed as a bit of a nerd with his awkward mannerisms and his thick horn rimmed glasses. In addition, Bruce had a major problem converting his thoughts, as well as his spoken words, back and forth between English and Chinese, and had a monumental complex about his small stature. Lastly, Bruce's most trying dilemma was that he had great difficulty adapting to the psychology of street survival in America, the guidelines of which were markedly different from those he had been accustomed to in Hong Kong.

Regarding Bruce's self image then, it is important to understand that in Hong Kong in the 1950s, kung fu practitioners were viewed as a notch above thugs. It was perhaps for this reason that Bruce arrived in this country with twenty pairs of shoes with Cuban heels and an equal number of suits, and that he longed for a sports car to "polish his image."

Throughout his life it is indisputable that Bruce placed an extremely high value on money. When he first arrived in Seattle, although he honestly believed that he could make $30,000 a year cranking out kung fu movies in Hong Kong, and he would often talk about wanting to one day be the greatest kung fu practitioner in the world, what he really wanted was to become a rich Hollywood movie star.

Not surprisingly, Glover's insights aptly identified the psychological profile of this young Chinese man who had spent the last eighteen years in foreign-occupied, refugee-saturated Hong Kong. Common to many was the fear and uncertainty, the resultant anger from racial hostility, the lack of self-identity from being lost in the panic-stricken masses, and the ultimate obsessive need to control every aspect of one's environment.

When Bruce first arrived in the United States, he felt that in his personal art of Wing Chun he had not progressed beyond the level of advanced beginner. Consequently, in the early 1960s he viewed himself as an unknown Chinese kung fu practitioner in America pitted against the well established Japanese and Korean trained martial arts community. If we add to that the undercurrent of racial tension that existed at that time and the fact that Bruce had not yet even reached the age of twenty, then it is readily understandable how he could have been fraught with reservations. Ironically, regarding his martial art, this may have been the only time in Bruce's life when he displayed any real degree of humility.

Shortly after Bruce arrived in Seattle, he began training with a man named Fook Young, an instructor at the Chinese Youth Club. In exchange for Wing Chun lessons, Young taught Bruce a form called Jeet Kune and a variety of styles, including Pak-Kua and the Preying Mantis. Supplemental to this training with Young, Bruce also began studying judo under the United States national champion Shuzo Kato, and trained in the Choy Li Fut school of kung fu with Richard Leong.

While living in Seattle, Bruce spent considerable time perusing the bookstores in Seattle's Chinatown and travel ing to Canada in search of texts on the martial arts. Within a year he had amassed an impressive library on the vast spectrum of eastern fighting arts. Following an exhaustive study, however, Bruce concluded that there were no real masters, and he took it as a personal insult. Many individuals who were close to Bruce throughout his life felt that his early obsessive search for what he perceived as a true martial arts master was fueled by his unfulfilled relationship with his father.

It was around this time, in the early 1960s, that Bruce began what would become a lifelong quest to form his own system of martial art. Leaving no stone unturned, he extended his study into the fields of wrestling, boxing, savate, karate and fencing, to list the most prominent.

In his book Unlimited Power, Anthony Robbins states: "The movers and shakers of the world are often professional modelers—people who have mastered the art of learning everything they can by following other people's experience rather than their own." And further: "To model excellence, you should become a detective, an investigator, someone who asks lots of questions and tracks down all the clues to what produces excellence." Throughout his life, one of Bruce Lee's greatest assets was that he fully understood this principle.

Bruce always claimed that he hated Ruby Chow's Chinese restaurant because he felt she exploited cheap Chinese labor, when in reality the simple fact was that he felt that he was above washing dishes for minimum wage. In his eyes Bruce had been a child movie star and quasi-popular gangster in Hong Kong. If for no other reason, he felt that because of Ruby's closeness to his mother, she would treat him as an honored guest while he pursued his education and other interests. Over time Bruce came to hate the sight of Ruby and her restaurant, and for the past thirty years Ruby's sole comment regarding Bruce Lee has been the same no matter who asks. "I was always taught that if you can't say something nice about someone, don't say anything at all."

Beginning in the late 1950s, Bruce began teaching kung fu to a small group of students. At that time, his small following wasn't collectively paying enough in dues to financially support a commercial school, and so they met informally at local public parks and recreation facilities.

Scholastically, at Edison Tech High School Bruce maintained a 2.6 grade point average and eventually entered the University of Washington after acquiring his high school diploma at the age of twenty. Not long after entering the University, he fell head over heels for a pretty Japanese girl named Amy Sanbo.

Small in stature and still strikingly beautiful, Amy reflected on her painful early childhood when she and her family had been interned by the United States government at the beginning of World War II.

"I still have vivid memories of Camp Tule Lake, and it was not a pleasant place at all. I didn't stop having nightmares until I was ten, dreams about the tanks coming through in the middle of the night and soldiers pointing guns at me when I was three. I remember people dying. A man dead and his wife stuffing a towel into his throat where he had been cut from ear to ear." Amy's eyes drifted to a portrait of her father that hung near the mahogany bookcase. "At night my father would play Beethoven's Sixth Symphony, which is the Pastorale. Although the family was allowed to take only two trunks to the internment camp, he

Amy Sanbo

filled them with his records and the Harvard classics. And so I would go to sleep to Beethoven's Sixth Symphony while my father read me Thoreau."

After the war ended, Amy and her family lived on Vashon Island for a brief period and then moved to Bellevue. These were estates for which Amy's father was the caretaker. After her father's death, Amy and her sister were taken to Seattle by their mother. "I guess you could say we lived in what today would be called a ghetto. It used to get very lively at night, and the police cars would be out there and you'd hear the screaming voices of prostitutes who worked the streets."

Amy recalled the first time she met Bruce Lee. "I was sitting in the HUB (Student Union Building) and I kept noticing that this Asian fellow kept moving his place closer and closer to where we were sitting. Anyway, I had to go to class and so I was walking past him and he suddenly reached up and grabbed my arm and with his thumb he pressed with such force I thought I was going to die and my knees buckled and I dropped my books on the floor and I said, 'Let go of me before I really get angry!' He did, and I asked him why he had grabbed me like that, and he said he was just showing his friend something or other. I had no idea what he was saying. I was just in pain. And it lasted for a week, I mean he had left a bruise there. And I thought to myself, 'what a complete jerk!' and I turned and walked away.

"Over the next few weeks Bruce kept appearing from out of nowhere," Amy continued. "And he'd say, 'How do you feel? Are you okay? My name is Bruce Lee.' And he was so persistent. He would bring up any subject just to talk to me."

Throughout his life, perhaps Bruce's greatest charac

ter flaw was that he found it utterly impossible to apologize to anyone. Nevertheless, he often found other ways to make amends, which had been the case with his earlier assault on Amy.

"I had injured my ankle during dance practice, and as a result had to walk on crutches for a week," Amy smiled as she shook her head in disbelief. "And in order to get to school in the morning, I had to walk through the parking lot and then across 23rd Avenue and then up this unbelievable flight of 367 concrete stairs north of the football stadium. It was really quite a trek. And then one morning Bruce appeared, picked me up off my feet and carried me, my books, my crutches and my heavy coat all the way to the top of those stairs! It was not only quite a feat, it was a grand gesture. And he did this every day for the entire week I was on crutches. And it wasn't only those stairs. After school he carried me to the third floor of my apartment and anywhere else he thought would be a problem for me. I think this more than made up for him bruising my arm.

"More than anything else, what I liked most about Bruce was that he never apologized for being Oriental," Amy recalled. "Back then most of the Asian fellows did apologize. I mean they took a secondary stance to all the whites, and it was enraging to me. Bruce was so cocky that it was refreshing. He was an Asian. He had this Asian face and it was similar to mine and he didn't apologize for it, and I like that."

Amy reminisced about the time when Bruce, a man rarely intimidated by anyone, crossed paths with the internationally renowned Theodore Roethke. "Well, here's this great Theodore Roethke, a Pulitzer Prize winner, and Bruce and I are sitting alone studying in Roethke's classroom at the University. Now you have to understand that Theodore Roethke was the only instructor in the English department who actually had his own classroom. And so in walks Roethke—a man so huge that he often described himself as a bear in his poems—and he says 'I'm Roethke, the poet! You are in my room!' I was in total shock and I though, 'Roethke, my God!' And I was enough of a student to back off and think 'Okay, I'll bow down. I'll keep quiet.' But Bruce didn't flinch at all. He stood up and walked right up to Roethke and stuck out his hand and said, 'I'm Bruce Sifu Lee,' with the emphasis on Sifu, 'kung fu master.' My God, I was ready to crawl out under the door, and I was hoping that Roethke hadn't caught a glimpse of me. I guess I was in a daze for a while, and then the next thing I remember is looking up and seeing Bruce standing at the blackboard with a chalk in his hand, lecturing to Roethke who is sitting in a front row chair! And Bruce is explaining to this Pulitzer Prize winning poet the essentials of kung fu and he's drawing Chinese characters all over Roethke's blackboard. And so for the next half-hour I stood there absolutely fascinated watching Bruce Lee captivate, if not mesmerize, Theodore Roethke and thinking, 'Oh my God, this is totally and completely bizarre!' This was in 1961, Bruce's first year at the University. The two never saw each other again, and sadly the great poet died two years later. And almost exactly ten years later, Bruce died."

Amy has been a gifted and widely acclaimed dance choreographer for going on three decades. She recalled her initial impressions of Bruce.

"At the time, Bruce watched the way the blacks moved because they were such great dancers, and Bruce had been crowned the cha-cha champion of Hong Kong. And so he would watch the blacks. And I would see him watching the way they walked down the street. I think he would just mimic them in the beginning, and then soon he developed his own unique expression. But whatever the end result, I remember thinking there's something about this man. He's unusual, and I saw it in his movement."

Earlier Amy had used the term kinetic genius to describe Bruce's unique talent. "Kinetic genius, that's exactly what Bruce was," she sat up briskly. "I mean he would be able to just look at a movement and assimilate it, absorb it, become that movement. I've been a dancer all my life, and I've always been intimately familiar with movement. And I was instantly aware that Bruce moved in a way that no other Asians moved.

"I'm horribly attracted to talent, and I could see that Bruce was extremely talented, although there was an awful lot of stuff that came out of his mouth that was just plain insufferable. But the point is, we were both addicted to movement. It was what we both physically liked to do. As a dancer, when I perform it's almost orgasmic. In a way it is very sexual, and I understood that in some ways Bruce was like that, too. And then sometimes after I'd worked out or he'd worked out, it was just so pleasant to be with someone who shared this intense love and understanding of movement."

Amy drifted into thought for a long pensive moment, trying to find the words. "From the beginning Bruce was open and honest about a problem he had sexually. We talked about it, and I said, 'Oh, I understand. That's not a problem.' But in my own head I was thinking, 'He does have a problem.' But it was nice that we had discussed it openly, and I think he felt comfortable that I was willing to work with him on this, although as time went on it became more of a problem than either of us may have felt it was initially."

Although Amy did not understand the cause of Bruce's casual attitude toward sex, which often appeared to her as symptomatic of male impotence, she had inadvertently stumbled upon his uncorrected childhood cryptorchidism that, as a credit to Bruce's straightforward nature, he often mentioned to people not long after making their acquaintance.

Amy's close friend Lonny, who knew Bruce when they were attending the University of Washington, elaborated. "Of course, the charming thing about Bruce was that he would tell you about all the things that would be embarrassing to anyone else. He had this childlike openness that at times was truly refreshing. Of course, years later when he returned to Hong Kong, all this changed."

"It was as if he just couldn't help being so honest about everything," Amy recalled. "Sometimes he would see me and he would break out into this silly grin and he'd be giddy and I thought it was so charming. Then other times he would become so involved with something that he would absolutely giggle. And I'd notice that he was wearing a nice shirt and say, 'That looks good on you, Bruce,' and he would giggle and say, 'You think so? Really?' And one morning he would see Lonny and say, 'Today I think Amy likes me eighty percent.' Then the next day he would say, 'I think it's sixty percent Roger and maybe forty percent me,' and everyday he would quote his percentages, and it was wonderfully amusing."

These were unquestionably the best years of Bruce's life. Only here does one find the fond memories of him

The University of Washington campus

teaching kung fu to little Chinese kids at the Chinese Baptist Church; evenings in his tiny, windowless apartment cooking his beloved oyster beef and noodles; the long walks by the lake. This was the only simple life Bruce would ever know, perhaps because these were the substance-free years and before money and stardom allowed ego to manifest itself. Perhaps it was because for the first time in his adolescent-adult years he was not living the life of a street gang member in Hong Kong.

Chapter Two

It was around this time that Bruce began to propose marriage to Amy on an almost daily basis. Having recognized her love of literature, he began writing love poems to her and recited romantic poetry to her from the Chinese classics. After giving Amy a ring that had once belonged to his grandmother, Bruce arranged to have his aunt, Eva Tso, whom he often referred to as his mother, fly to the United States specifically to meet his bride-to-be.

"All this made me extremely uncomfortable because Bruce never mentioned to me that this woman was coming to meet me," Amy recalled. "And, you see, in the Oriental custom, getting the approval of a close relative is just one step away from the actual ceremony. The whole thing made me very uneasy because I still had much to do in my life. I wanted more than home economics and children, and I thought Bruce understood this. But still he kept pressing."

Because of her childhood interment, Amy has throughout her life been sympathetic to those less fortunate than herself, which was something Bruce would have been wise to consider when he proposed that he and Amy take up residence in Hong Kong. "I saw documentaries on Hong Kong and what I saw was appalling, you know the boat people, the city looked crowded," Amy said. "It looked uncared for and it was like poverty had just taken over. And I said to Bruce I don't know if I could handle that. It would just distress me. And he said we didn't have to be there, that I didn't have to see that part of it. I mean it's all around you, right. He said, no, we'd live in a mansion on Victoria Peak and look down at the city, like in The World of Suzy Wong. I said, 'No I can't live like that. I can't ignore those people on the boat. They're in poverty, Bruce. And I can't feel comfortable living up on some hill with servants. I can't deal with that."

It is difficult to understand why Bruce felt it necessary to offer Amy a lavish lifestyle that he unquestionably could not afford. In a sense many felt he was living the life of The Great Gatsby.

"You see, Amy's partly an inner-city person," Lonny interjected. "And when you're talking about Bruce living in the overcrowded conditions on Nathan Road above the row of shops, there's a correlation because Amy lived in the ghetto since her mother was widowed and worked cleaning houses. And so maybe that was familiar to Bruce and we didn't recognize that, and of course all the time that he was implying all this family wealth back in Hong Kong he was living in a tiny room on the third floor of Ruby Chow's."

"It was more than the stark differences in our social awareness," Amy reminisced. "I remember one day near the end Bruce asked me what he could do that would win me over, and I thought about it for a long moment, and I said quite honestly, 'match my grades.' I guess what turned me off eventually was that Bruce was not as broadly educated as I was, and that he was fixated on just the physical aspect of life."

There was the far greater problem of Bruce wanting Amy to follow the Asian tradition and live out her life as his devoted lotus blossom. The subject matter brought a rush of color to Amy's face. "I was not about to be subservient to Bruce, despite his demands. But it was a constant battle. If a woman wasn't independent enough to continually speak her mind, he would oppress her even more. This was his temperament. Whereas I felt I had the upper hand with him because I didn't allow any of that. Other than if he were to beat me senseless, but then I would have shot him. He was one who believed that women were to be used, and he always quoted that lyric from The King and I about the bee going from flower to flower and petal to petal, and so he was a real classic macho pig, he really was. And it used to offend me, and I wrote him back a poem, not in four-meter like he used to do in Chinese poems, but I wrote him a long lengthy poem about what I thought about him, and I thought if he could figure it out, good, more power to him, but I figured that he couldn't. No, I wasn't trying to be unclear, I was very clear."

Amy felt there was more to Bruce's machoism than his Far Eastern upbringing. "Bruce carried a lot of pain inside him and a great deal of anger as a result of being emotionally scarred in his childhood. I felt that it was from his father's rejection and his fixation on his son Peter rather than Bruce. But he never really talked about his father. He'd mention his mother, but he wouldn't talk about his father. And whenever anyone would ask about his brother Peter, Bruce would totally avoid the subject."

The break up did not go smoothly, and ultimately Amy departed for New York where she had taken a summer job in preparation for the 1964 New York World's Fair, instructing her mother and friends not to tell Bruce of her whereabouts. "I just felt that it was over between us and I knew that Bruce was an extremely obsessive person. He had displayed this characteristic throughout our relationship. He was not someone who was going to be denied. And he was persistent enough, and even childish enough, to pursue me at all costs. And I didn't know if I could have dealt with it."

Bruce returned to Hong Kong in some disarray, having seen his romance with Amy Sanbo dissolve. At that time

Hong Kong had recently suffered another mass influx of refugees from Communist China. Shantytowns had sprung up, families built shelters on the roofs of buildings and people slept in parks and on the street. The drought that summer did not make things any easier. The water was on only a few hours every fourth day. Nevertheless, Bruce managed to enjoy his brief stay. He went swimming at the sand beaches, went to the movies, visited amusement parks, ate in restaurants, or simply soaked up the atmosphere and energy of the bustling streets. While there Bruce continued some serious training with Yip Man and had a brief affair with his childhood sweetheart Pak Yan.

With the summer coming to an end, Bruce returned to Seattle where he resumed his daily life at the University and his nightly job at Ruby Chow's. Although he kept up his obsessive search for Amy, she couldn't be found. Across the boards nothing seemed to be working. There was no future in school, which was more than evident when in the fall quarter he failed, of all classes, Introductory Modern Chinese.

Empathetic to Bruce's circumstances, Taky Kimura, one of Bruce's first students in Seattle, arranged for Bruce's students to pay enough in monthly dues so that Bruce could quit his job bussing tables and move into his own apartment. If nothing else, he would no longer have to endure Ruby's incessant complaining about his wooden dummy that he often pounded on behind the restaurant.

Over the next few months Bruce stepped up his schedule of public demonstrations and, as a result, student enrollment gradually increased. With the added revenue, Bruce signed a commercial lease on a small building that soon became the home of the Jun Fan Gung Fu Institute.

Chapter Two

Just prior to opening the Institute, Bruce met a girl named Linda Emery, who had just graduated from Garfield High School where she had not only excelled scholastically, but had also been a member of the varsity diving team and a school cheerleader. Linda was a blonde, blue-eyed Caucasian girl, born and raised in Seattle by a mother with strict religious values. Linda had previously dated a young man who was half-Japanese, and her mother became incensed upon learning about the courtship. Subsequently, upon entering her freshman year at the University of Washington, over the next several months Linda began to occasionally see Bruce without her mother's knowledge.

Bruce's newly established Jun Fan Gung Fu Institute was short-lived, due mostly to a high turnover of students. Eventually Bruce was unable to pay the rent, and the school was closed.

Realizing that he was about to fail out of school and that he again had no visible means of support, Bruce began traveling to Oakland on weekends, primarily to spend time with a kung fu practitioner named James Lee. The two men had been introduced a year earlier and were considering opening a kung fu school together. It was around this time, in the winter of 1963, that James drove Bruce to Los Angeles to meet black belt kenpoist Ed Parker, who was in the initial planning stages of the first nationwide martial arts tournament scheduled for the following summer in Long Beach.

After three years at the University, Bruce failed to accumulate enough credits to advance beyond the status of freshman, and he dropped out at the end of the spring 1964 quarter. Literally flat broke and without a job, he sold his car and moved into James Lee's home in Oakland, with no plans of returning to Seattle.

On August 2, 1964 Bruce appeared at the International Karate Championships, which were held at the Long Beach Municipal Auditorium. This was the first major karate tournament in the United States, and it was an overwhelming success. Paramount to all else was the heartfelt camaraderie that embraced the entire assemblage of martial artists who had come from all parts of the country to perform and compete. Sunday evening was the grand finale, which featured the final sparring matches. The event had been sold out for months, and nearly a thousand people were turned away at the door. Never before had the public seen this kind of action fight competition. Hawaiian-born Mike Stone in a sudden-death tie-breaking point won the grand championship, and the suspense and adrenaline pump was unbelievable.

There were many demonstrations that evening. Jhoon Rhee, who stood 5'5", gave an incredible display of aerial kicking, shattering pine boards held seven feet in the air. Later, Ben Largusa thrilled the audience with a performance of the Filipino deadly stick-fighting art of escrima. Takyuki Kubota demonstrated what Black Belt Magazine later called "shocking feats," and eight-year-old Roy Castro, the son of renowned Bay Area black belt Ralph Castro, gave a demonstration that brought the crowd to its feet with resounding applause.

It was amid this grand spectacle that Bruce Lee, a relatively unknown kung fu practitioner from Hong Kong, walked onto the main floor with his advanced student Taky Kimura. Bruce wore a black uniform and these strange black boots, and Taky resembled something from another planet with his padded suit of body armor, shin guards and what looked like a catcher's mask over his face.

Chapter Two

Although initially it was the blinding speed of his hands and kicks that captured everyone's attention, it was Bruce's aggressive and witty personality that many were still recalling months later. Arrogant. Cocky. Self-assured. At times outright brazen. In an uncanny way, Bruce's overall personality was surprisingly similar to that of the celebrated and flamboyant Muhammad Ali. And like Ali, despite Bruce's arrogance, one had to root for him. There was something about this explosive young man from Hong Kong. He had something most martial arts students were struggling to achieve. He seemingly had this unadorned inner confidence, and he appeared to be absolutely fearless.

In sharp contrast to what was inaccurately depicted in MCA's movie Dragon, Bruce did not compete in the sparring competition, nor did he issue a full contact challenge match to any and all present. Not only would such savage behavior been insulting to the martial arts community, but Ed Parker would have never allowed such a violent public display, and Bruce Lee had too much class to have even considered such nonsense.

Two weeks after appearing at the Long Beach Internationals, Bruce returned to Seattle. Depending on which biographer's version one reads, this week of Bruce's life can be anything from warmly uplifting to painfully frustrating. In any case, what we do know is that he arrived in Seattle in the second week of August 1964, and that on August 12 he and Linda Emery appeared at the King County courthouse and applied for a marriage license, with plans of eloping.

Two days later Linda's mother read about her daughter's impending marriage in the vital statistics column of the local newspaper. Furious, she climbed to the third floor of

Sears and Roebuck, where Linda had taken a summer job, and shook the paper in her daughter's face. "Is this you?"

That evening Bruce and Linda were called in on the family carpet. This was the first time that Linda's family had met Sifu Bruce Jun Fan Lee, and they demanded an explanation. Besides her mother and stepfather (Linda's father had died when she was four), Linda's favorite uncle, an extremely pious man, began quoting chapter and verse. This was not the Christian thing to do, this mixing of the races. There would be hell to pay, for everyone.

Bruce interrupted, "I want to marry your daughter. I'm Chinese, by the way."

Perhaps they had mistaken him for Japanese and thrown him into the post-WWII anti-Japanese racist hysteria. They hadn't. All Asians were taboo. Caucasians, especially those with the last name of Emery, married Caucasians.

They argued well into the night and throughout the next day. As far as Linda's family was concerned, Linda had just turned nineteen and was too young. Why couldn't they wait a year? Besides, Linda didn't know how to cook and clean. What troubled everyone was that it appeared that Bruce had no visible means of support, which was true. Apart from the racial and familial elements of this meeting, which have been widely reported over the years, the real issue facing the Emery family was that Linda was nearly four months pregnant, and of course back then if you got a girl pregnant, you married her, plain and simple.

Although unaware of the pregnancy, Amy Sanbo did recall sensing that something was terribly wrong when she returned to Seattle for a brief visit with her family. "I felt sorry for Linda. I remember seeing them in October walk ing through Chinatown. It was cold, and she was wearing a big coat. You know there's a way that you walk together when you're in love, or if you're boyfriend and girlfriend there's a lift to you, but she didn't. She looked like she was just pulled in like she was terribly unhappy. And I felt sorry for her because I had already made up my mind that I knew what living with Bruce day to day was going to be like, and so she was going to face that and I felt very sorry for her. And I remember feeling pretty bad for her when Bruce died and the reports that he had mistresses and all sorts of things began to surface. Again I felt almost empathy or sympathy for Linda. Because of the lifestyle she had to live with Bruce, I'm sure she was miserable."

In less than twenty-four hours Linda and Bruce were married in a church service that was speedily arranged by Linda's mother. Besides Linda's mother and grandmother, the rest of the Emery clan boycotted the service, which ended with Bruce's newly acquired mother-in-law grumbling that her newly acquired son-in-law "could have at least brought flowers." A short time later Linda moved to Oakland where she and Bruce shared a bedroom in the home of James Lee.

Even after the marriage Bruce continued to search for Amy Sanbo and would call her friends and family saying, "Where's Amy? I need to talk to her." Finally, when Amy married in the fall of 1964, the calls stopped.

Why the persistence? Why this sense of utter desperation surrounding Bruce's unrelenting pursuit of Amy? "The most important thing that Bruce ever said to me," Amy paused to gather her thoughts, "and this was perhaps the first time he was really truly honest, was, he looked deep into my eyes and said, 'You know, you're really mature, you're different from the rest.' I think that Bruce felt safe with me because I kept a strong hand on him. There was a strange side of Bruce that always set up a situation, or treated a situation, so that the other person had no choice but to retaliate and react with anger. In a peculiar way Bruce seemed to gain pleasure from this, although other times it seemed to frighten him. Looking back, I believe that very early Bruce saw himself becoming a loose cannon and he sensed a wisdom in me that was almost parental."

Academy award winning screenwriter Stirling Silliphant, himself a black belt, several decades later sadly reminisced. "The martial arts never did for Bruce what they did for me or other people. Bruce never achieved any calm out of the martial arts. The very thing that should have protected him, didn't. He invited a lot of the slings that kept coming back at him. There's enough trouble in life. Most of us duck it... At times Bruce seemed to welcome it."

CHAPTER 3

Hollywood

"Well," said Monkey, "years ago a first-class Zen adept taught me the art of having one's head cut off. I don't know whether I can remember it or not, but I am quite willing to experiment."

• 'Monkey' by Wu Ch'eng-en

Bruce's newly established kung fu institute in Oakland had barely opened when Bruce received an open challenge from a kung fu practitioner named Wong Jak Man. Since Bruce's death in July 1973, the fight details have been widely reported by Linda Lee through leading martial arts magazines. Besides James Lee, who died before the story became truly newsworthy, the only other eye witnesses to the battle were Wong Jak Man and a handful of his followers, none of whom have ever had any self-interest in the subsequent two decades of capitalizing on the Lee legend.

It is true that Wong Jak Man personally instigated the confrontation, claiming that he was representing a group of martial arts elders who resided nearby in San Francisco's Chinatown. What has always been puzzling, however, is what had angered these elders, if they were angered at all?

As the story goes, sometime in January 1963 Wong Jak Man arrived at Bruce's Oakland school and allegedly came straight to the point—Bruce Lee had been revealing the secrets of kung fu to non-Chinese! As a historical note, it is interesting that just a short while before this now infamous confrontation between Bruce Lee and Wong Jak Man, all but a stone's throw away in Los Angeles rising kenpoist Ed Parker had just published, without incident or complaint, his popular hardback book titled The Secrets of Chinese Karate. And although Parker was Hawaiian and perhaps couldn't be held accountable for teaching non-Orientals, his associate instructor in the Los Angeles karate school, the legendary Tai Chi master Jimmy Wu, taught non-Chinese on a daily basis without ever being held accountable by any Chinese elders, kung fu masters or anyone else.

Perhaps an alternate explanation has to do with territorial infringement. It has been reported that years earlier members of a local triad came to Bruce's Seattle school demanding money. Triad Oath #27 may have had something to do with both the Seattle and Oakland encounters: "I must not trespass upon the territory occupied by my sworn brothers. I shall be killed by five thunderbolts if I pretend to have no knowledge of my brothers' rights in such matters."

Whatever the reason behind Wong Jak Man's visit, Bruce was handed a written ultimatum allegedly stating that he either cease teaching non-Orientals or accept Wong's challenge to open combat. Having agreed to fight rather than close his school, Bruce suddenly became incensed when Wong suggested that they simply spar lightly for a few minutes. "I'm not standing for any of that!" Lee fumed. "You've made the challenge, so I'm making the rules! So as far as I'm concerned, it's no-holds-barred—it's all out!"

Steadfastly denying reports that the fight ended in a draw, Linda Lee has for over two decades claimed that the surprisingly inelegant battle was over in a "matter of minutes." Neither participant received any substantial injuries, although the experience led Bruce to later conclude that much of his martial art was ineffective and that, because he had too quickly become winded during the confrontation, he needed to do some serious work on his cardiovascular system.

One month later in Hong Kong, Bruce's father died of a heart attack at the age of sixty-four. At the time, Bruce was in the U.S., and he immediately boarded a plane for Hong Kong. Upon entering the funeral parlor to pay his last respects, and according to Chinese custom, it was required that he crawl to his father's coffin. That Bruce did this, wailing as he went, is perhaps evidence of the deep emotional hurt he had buried throughout his life for the father who had remained distant and whom Bruce could never please.

A major turning point in Bruce's life occurred in August 1964 when Ed Parker captured on film Bruce's impressive kung fu demonstration at the Long Beach Karate Internationals. When subsequently the footage was shown to television producer William Dozier, Bruce was cast in Dozier's new series The Green Hornet, which began shooting in June of 1966. Van Williams starred in the role of Britt Reed (The Green Hornet), based on the 1950s radio series character who was a crusading, crime-busting newspaper man. Bruce played the Hornet's trusted servant Kato, who was an adept in the deadly art of kung fu.

In 1967 Bruce Lee went virtually unnoticed in the martial arts world. Although he had gained some popularity as Kato, to martial artists the true heroes were the tournament champions best known as the golden boys of a bygone era—Joe Lewis, Chuck Norris, and Mike Stone. Of the three, Lewis spent the most time with Bruce.

Back then there was no one on the tournament circuit more lethal than Joe Lewis. Not only was he lightening fast and had a punching power that could seemingly shatter a bank vault, he was notorious for a temper so explosive that on occasion Ed Parker had to physically restrain him from tearing his competitor limb-from-limb.

By aligning himself with Joe Lewis, Bruce stood to gain the recognition he so passionately desired. According to Lewis, Bruce wanted the prestige of being able to claim the rank of master, and he would back this up by displaying his students who were national champions. At the time Bruce was in his late twenties, and, if for no other reason, because of his age the kung fu hierarchy wasn't about to recognize him as a master of anything, let alone show him any respect. This angered Bruce and he began to boil.

Soon after The Green Hornet began airing, Bruce, now a television celebrity, began granting interviews to various martial arts magazines in which he began unleashing his wrath at the martial arts community at large, specifically targeting what he alleged was a preponderance of self-proclaimed, ill-qualified masters. Well known for his directness, Bruce openly accused many of these martial arts icons of being inexcusably out of shape and often went as far as calling many of them outright fakes.

Whatever it was these masters were teaching, presumably eighteen centuries of highly guarded, secret knowledge, Bruce stated publicly with great fervor that 90 percent of it was baloney!

Totally outraged, respected black belts in the martial arts community, both in the U.S. and the Far East, accused Bruce of being nothing more than a disrespectful upstart, while others went as far as to label him a young punk with a big mouth. Undaunted, Bruce openly challenged his critics to "prove themselves." Often, in an incredibly bold gesture, Bruce would single out a particular martial artist and, standing directly in front of the man and within striking range, would defy him to "try to hit me." Unbelievably, none who tried could. Generally speaking, Bruce was an embarrassment to the martial arts community, who simply had no idea what to do with him and at the same time couldn't shut him up.

Fundamentally there was really no great mystery to much of Bruce's talent. As a foundation he was an incredible natural athlete, "one in two billion," to quote Ed Parker, and he kept himself in superb physical condition, which he worked at to the point of clinical obsession. Additionally, as for unrestricted open combat, he had simplified his art and perfected several key elements that often proved to be devastating.

From the great fencing master Julio Martinez Castello, Bruce mastered the ability of opening and closing the gap, or distance, between him and his opponent, to the degree that he could strike with the speed of a cobra. Second, Bruce also mastered what Castello taught as "broken-rhythm," which is one's ability to become enmeshed with, and thereby disrupt, his opponent's natural rhythm. Once perfected, a man normally slower than his opponent can win by striking his adversary on the half and quarter beats. The total effect was both highly confusing and monumentally frustrating.

Moreover, Bruce had become so skilled in the art of western boxing that many were convinced that he could have stepped into the ring with any professional boxer in his own weight division and most likely the next higher division as well. When Bruce closed the gap, most martial artists were often completely dumbfounded because they were not accustomed to teeing up with a boxer of Bruce's professional skill.

Similarly, Bruce was equally dangerous at a distance, for he could kick his opponent from head to toe with the blinding speed of a bullwhip and, quite literally, with the power of a horse. Moreover, he had perfected the art of kicking his opponent's front shin as speedily and effectively as a boxer uses a jab. Not only was this unnervingly distracting, but it severely hampered his opponent's interest in either kicking his own front leg or advancing. . . . .

Unquestionably Bruce's greatest asset was that he was a master at instantly discerning his opponent's weaknesses. A short time after Bruce moved to Los Angeles, he began recruiting students from the ranks of Ed Parker's brown and black belt classes. The growing exodus of Parker's advanced students did not sit well with the godfather of kenpo.

Bruce readily identified the inherent problem that flustered many of Parker's advanced kenpo students. Essentially the problem was threefold. The first issue facing the kenpo practitioner was that the lion's share of his learned techniques were defenses against an opponent who attacked by stepping through with his right leg from back to front as he delivered a locked out straight right punch. The problem, which Bruce smugly pointed out, was that no street-fighter he ever encountered fought like this. The second issue was that Bruce refused to stand still while a kenpoist worked on him as if he were a stationary mannequin. Instead he was quick and elusive. Lastly, kenpo students were primarily trained to move to the outside of an attacking opponent. Because one of Bruce's main objectives was always to control the center line (much like the winning chess player controls the center of the board, and the winning basketball team controls the lane) there just wasn't any way to get Bruce Lee into this alignment because he would continuously maneuver himself in such a way that he was facing you head-on. In stark contrast, Bruce effortlessly, if not magically, could quickly get to the outside of his opponent where he then blasted away. That left the inside, toe-to-toe. Unfortunately for Lee's opponent, this was where Bruce was at his best. Being a skilled technician of chi sao, or sticking hands, Bruce could handily defeat an opponent standing inside this range, and he could do it blindfolded!

In defense of the art of kenpo and its students, Ed Parker was a man of great insight. Over the years, many kenpo defectors have returned to resume their study, having discovered the truth of what Parker had been saying for years—that what worked for Bruce Lee was not only unique to Bruce but would have almost assuredly get most martial artists in serious trouble.

By the summer of 1966, Bruce and Linda (along with their son Brandon who was born February 1, 1965) had moved from Oakland to West Los Angeles, where they lived in a high-rise residential complex called the Barrington Plaza. One of the owners of the complex was Don Karnes. Himself a student of martial arts, Karnes soon befriended

Bruce. Perhaps here Karnes should be acknowledged for making one of the most important contributions to Bruce's life.

Of the nearly two thousand books in his vast library, Bruce valued a particular text above all others, and he used to read it constantly. The book was Think and Grow Rich by Napoleon Hill, which was given to him by Don Karnes,

Barrington Plaza

along with his conviction that if Bruce would diligently and steadfastly follow the doctrines outlined in Hill's book, life would grant him anything and everything he requested. Not long after receiving Think and Grow Rich, and following its precepts, Bruce wrote what he wanted from life and what he was willing to give back in return:

"My Chief Personal Aim In Life"

I, Bruce Lee, will be the highest paid Oriental superstar in the United States. In return I will give the most exciting performances and render the best of quality in the capacity of an actor. Starting in 1970, I will achieve world fame and from then onward till the end of 1980 I will have in my possession the sum of $10,000,000 - then I will live the way I please and achieve inner harmony and happiness.

Unfortunately, the almighty Nielsen ratings had not been kind to The Green Hornet. Following the airing of twenty-six episodes during the 1966-67 television season, the show was canceled for poor ratings, the result of which plunged Bruce into a marked depression.

Closing the door to his dressing room at Twentieth Century Fox, Bruce reluctantly resumed teaching his elite clique of private students who could pay his $275 hourly rate, never again to return to public instruction. By now Lee's student roster was comprised almost exclusively of Hollywood and sports celebrities and included Lee Marvin, James Coburn, Elke Sommer, Roman Polanski, Joe Hyams, Steve McQueen, James Garner, producer Sy Weintraub, basketball star Kareem Abdul-Jabbar, and academy award win

One of Bruce Lee's elite students, James Coburn

ning screenwriter Stirling Silliphant.

From the beginning Bruce was enamored with the Hollywood crowd and soon began to appear at various parties and social gatherings. His presence was short lived, however, for he found it difficult fitting in.

Over the years Bruce has been quoted as having said, "I don't drink or smoke and these events are many times senseless. I don't like to wear stuffy clothes and be at places where everyone is trying to impress each other. I'm not saying I'm modest. I just rather like to be around a few friends and talk informally about boxing and the martial arts." Although undoubtedly Bruce did say this, the statement is misleading. One of Bruce's closest friends observed that "Bruce was a voracious and non-stop talker, and the subjects always the same—Bruce Lee and kung fu. This could wear on even the most loyal of his friends and students." Peter Chin, who worked on the set of The Green Hornet, recalled that people were often put off by Bruce's behavior off screen. "He was always showing people his muscles, showing them how strong he was. After Bruce had walked away, you'd hear someone say, 'Oh, he's bullshitting—he's a big loudmouth.'"

With the cancellation of The Green Hornet, Bruce became interested in developing a starring role for himself that centered on a Shaolin priest wandering around the Midwestern United States in the 1800s. Ironically, Bruce learned that Warner Brothers had for some time been developing an identical concept with producer Fred Weintraub, which would inevitably become the runaway syndicated hit series Kung-Fu.

After months of developing the project with Fred Weintraub, Bruce was ultimately told that the starring role had been given to David Carradine, and that neither Warner Brothers nor ABC Television had ever seriously considered Bruce for the leading role because: (1) he was too short, (2) he was too Chinese, (3) he was too inexperienced, and (4) he wasn't a big enough name to sustain a weekly prime-time series.

Understandably Bruce was disappointed, for a while even despondent. Unfortunately he had long since developed a minorities complex about being Asian in the western-dominated industry and, as a result, ultimately became convinced that he was being held back from Hollywood stardom by racial barriers.

In an effort to turn the tide, Bruce attempted to develop a co-starring role for himself that would showcase his martial arts. In order to accomplish this, he solicited the help of two of his students, Steve McQueen, who would star in the film, and Stirling Silliphant, who would write it.

Excited over the prospect, Bruce and Stirling went to McQueen and offered him the starring role, only to have him turn it down. Speaking candidly, McQueen told Bruce that he wasn't in the business to make Bruce into a star, and that he wasn't interested in carrying him on his shoulders. Bruce was more than shocked. He was furious. Leaving McQueen's house with Stirling, he paused on the front lawn and shook his fist at the star's palatial home, angrily proclaiming that one day he would be a bigger star than McQueen!

Unbending, Bruce approached another one of his private students, James Coburn, and pitched him the basic story. Although Coburn would have star billing, Bruce would play five different martial arts characters. Clearly this was to be a vehicle for Bruce, and it is understandable why a star of McQueen's magnitude would have declined. Upon Coburn's expressed interest, and after several unacceptable drafts of Bruce's story by other writers, Stirling Silliphant inevitably took on the task of writing the script, which was now called The Silent Flute.

Steve McQueen's certificate from Bruce Lee

BRUCE LEE'S
TAO OF
CHINESE GUNG FU
振藩拳道

以無限為有限

以無法為有法

學生 McQueen 係 Calif 省 Los Angeles 縣人在館修練期滿准予升入第一級 此證

李振藩

一九六七年九月 日

Date Sept. 1967

This is to certify that

Steve McQueen

Is personally taught by Bruce Lee, and having fulfilled the necessary requirements, is hereby promoted to 1st. rank in Bruce Lee's Tao of Chinese Gung Fu.

Meanwhile, in March of 1969 Bruce was admitted to St. John's Hospital in Santa Monica where surgeons removed the undeveloped testicle that had remained undescended since birth and repaired a hernia. A year after Bruce's surgery to correct his cryptorchidism, and in a somewhat camouflaged but related matter, his overly publicized back ailment occurred.

According to Dr. Lionel Walpin, who examined Lee in September 1970, Bruce's back spasm was triggered during an episode of sexual intercourse in June 1970. After giving Bruce a complete physical examination and ordering a set of spinal X-rays, Dr. Walpin concluded that there was little wrong with him. After a brief period, and with the help of a Jacuzzi, Bruce straightened out and returned to his usual workouts and running.

Besides Dr. Walpin, Bruce was referred to Dr. Herbert Tanney by director Blake Edwards, who is best known for his string of "Pink Panther" movies and his marriage to actress/singer Julie Andrews.

The result of Bruce's meeting with Dr. Tanney was a general work-up, lab tests and spinal X-rays. Although nothing was seriously the matter with Bruce, Tanney, as he had been doing for a substantial time with Edwards, began injecting cortisone into Bruce's spine. Apparently it didn't completely remedy the problem, whatever the problem was, and in December 1970 Tanney referred Bruce to Dr. Ellis Silberman in Century City for another extensive series of X-rays. Silberman's summary: "Examination of the lumbosacral spine and pelvis was within normal limits." Bruce wasn't satisfied, and he continued to return to Tanney's office on a semi-regular basis for cortisone (depo-Medrol) injections.

Most noteworthy is the warning that is clearly displayed on the side of every bottle of depo-Medrol, as well as being written in the Physician's Desk Reference: "Therapy with depo-Medrol does not [prevent] the need for the conventional measures usually employed. Although this method of treatment will [improve] symptoms, it is in no sense a cure and the hormone has no effect on the cause of the inflammation." In simple lay terms this is a warning to the user that the habitual use of cortisone is akin to painting over rust.

There were other warnings listed by the drug manufacturer that are equally troublesome: "Psychic derangements may appear when cortisone is used, ranging from euphoria, insomnia, mood swings, personality changes, and severe depression to frank psychotic manifestations."

There would be more referrals. In March 1971, Bruce was again sent to specialist Dr. Lionel Walpin. Again, Walpin's impression was that "no specific diagnosis was suspected." In addition, more X-rays were taken by Dr. David Eisenstein, whose general conclusion was that Bruce had a normal thoracic spine.

Generally speaking, what Bruce had was tantamount to a large gnat buzzing around his face; a nuisance more than anything, and one that might continue to bother him periodically, as long as he persisted in his rigorous exercise and martial arts training regimens.

It was around this time that Stirling Silliphant submitted his final draft of The Silent Flute to Warner Brothers. The studio was impressed with Stirling's script, although they would only agree to fund the project if the film were shot in India where they had a sizeable amount of blocked rupees that could only be spent inside the country.

And so off they went—Bruce Lee, James Coburn, and Stirling Silliphant traipsing through India and Pakistan to scout locations.

Not long into their sojourn there was friction between Bruce and Coburn. To begin with, Bruce had taken to giving kung fu demonstrations that would invariably gather large crowds. This bothered Coburn, whose privacy was shattered once he was recognized by the crowd who had congregated around Bruce. To digress for a moment, it was during this trip that many photographs were taken of Bruce flying through the air in the middle of the Indian desert while demonstrating lockout side-kicks. Arguably this would have been an almost impossible feat had Bruce been afflicted with a crippling back injury.

In addition, Bruce had been in the habit of humming pop tunes under his breath and would often do this for hours while the three men were driving through the scorching desert. Finally, Coburn couldn't take it anymore, and he spun around and shouted at Bruce who was sitting in the back seat, "For Christ's sake, man, would you cut that out! You're driving me crazy!" Bruce said nothing, but when Coburn turned back around, he shook his fist at the star's back in the same manner as he had earlier done at McQueen's house.

Late that evening the three men checked into a hotel. Bruce felt affronted because Coburn had been given star-preference by the hotel staff, which resulted in Coburn having a more luxurious room. Furious, Bruce went to Stirling to complain that he was supposed to be the star of The Silent Flute, not Coburn, further adding that one day he would be the biggest movie star in the world—bigger than Coburn, whom he now added to his "I'll-show-you" list just below Steve McQueen!

This was not the first time something like this had happened. A month earlier Bruce had accompanied Coburn to Beverly Hills where the two men ended up at an expensive men's clothing store on Rodeo Drive. While Coburn was trying on Polo sweaters it suddenly occurred to him that the parking meter where his Ferrari was parked was running low. He turned to Bruce and asked if he would go outside and put another quarter in the meter. Bruce hardly uttered a word to Coburn for the rest of the day, and he often told the story as if he had a score to settle.

After months in the desert and upon their return to the states, Coburn refused to do the picture, stating that Bruce had no idea of the production problems, and that from an artistic perspective the picture should not be made in India. Bruce wouldn't listen. He desperately wanted the film made for emotional reasons, at all costs, and he didn't care where. According to Silliphant, in Bruce's eyes The Silent Flute was his only hope of breaking into Hollywood, and he simply would not let it go.

It didn't matter. With Coburn's refusal, Warner Brothers dropped out of the deal.

CHAPTER 4

The Big Boss and Fist of Fury

"When the Rolls Royce arrives, I know exactly what I'm going to do. I'm going to drive down to the waterfront and call Roman Polanski and Steve McQueen on the car phone. And when they ask where I'm calling from, I'll say from the back seat of my Rolls Royce overlooking the junks in Hong Kong harbor!"

Bruce Lee

March 1970 to April 1971 was one of the darkest periods of Bruce's life, and it was then that he began to display a placard on his desk telling all to Walk On! Besides having fallen into a depression over his stagnating acting career, Bruce was in serious financial trouble. Confident that his career had been launched with The Green Hornet, he had purchased an expensive home on Roscamere Drive in Bel Air and was now having difficulty making the mortgage payments.

In an effort to make ends meet, Linda began working

the night shift at an answering service for minimum hourly wage. To Bruce the fact that his wife had gone to work was a blow to his ego and, as a result, he and Linda concocted an elaborate network of excuses that would explain Linda's absence from the home. Beset with worry, Bruce soon traveled to Hong Kong in search of work in the Mandarin film industry and to arrange for his mother and brother to come live at his newly acquired house.

Upon his arrival at Kai Tak Airport, Bruce was amazed at his reception. Although The Green Hornet had ended its lackluster one season run in the states, reruns had played favorably in Hong Kong for months in syndication. Consequently, when Bruce arrived in Hong Kong, reporters requested interviews, and radio and television wanted him

Bruce's Bel Air home

for guest spots. Suddenly thrust back into the limelight, Bruce gave a spectacular kung fu demonstration on local television that would ultimately conspire with other factors to change his life forever.

In the early 1970s the Mandarin film industry was dominated by Run Run Shaw, who was more formally addressed as Sir Run Run Shaw, having been knighted by the queen. Born and raised in Shanghai, Run Run had fled to Hong Kong Island in the late 1940s and, with his brothers, formed Shaw Brothers, Ltd., which officially went public in 1958.

One of the company's biggest holdings was the illustrious "Movie Town," which was an enormous studio complex as powerful as MGM in its heyday. In addition, movie mogul Run Run also owned the lion's share of theaters throughout Southeast Asia and, as a result, controlled over 90 percent of all Far East distribution. Including Run Run's other investments, the entire family fortune was in 1971 estimated conservatively to be worth US$200 million and even as high as one billion.

While in Hong Kong, Bruce called his close boyhood friend Siu Kee Lun ("Unicorn") who was under contract to the Shaw Brothers and asked that he inquire whether Run Run might be interested in making Bruce an offer. Days later Unicorn called Bruce. Yes, Run Run seemed interested, and yes, he had heard of Bruce's lukewarm success in Hollywood and, well, all things considered, he was willing to offer Bruce the sum of US$75 per week if he would sign an exclusive seven-year contract.

Run Run's offer was not uncommon. Back then his contract players lived on the company lot in cement block dormitories and worked for low wages under primitive con ditions on long-term contracts, without any real unions, insurance, fringe or medical benefits.

Bruce broke into loud guffaws, then countered Shaw's offer, asking for HK$10,000 (US$2,100) for his services on one film only and no contract beyond that. Shaw never responded, and Bruce departed Hong Kong.

Mandarin film industry mogul, Run Run Shaw

While Bruce was traveling in the Far East, Stirling Silliphant wrote a part for him in a new series for Paramount Television called Longstreet. The lead role starred James Franciscus, who played a blind man ultimately led to enlightenment by Bruce's martial arts character. Upon his return from Hong Kong, Bruce shot the pilot episode of Longstreet, which would not air until after he had again departed for the Far East.

Born and raised in Shanghai, producer Raymond Chow (Chow Man-wai), who had left the employ of the Shaw Brothers following a bitter falling out, had formed Golden Harvest Films, which in 1971 was in such financial distress that many predicted the next typhoon would demolish the renegade studio's two ramshackle sound stages and blow their wafer-thin ledgers into the polluted harbor.

Raymond had been impressed with Bruce's televised kung fu demonstration and was even more impressed with the fact that Bruce had taken the time to view every martial arts film that had come out of Hong Kong in the past two years. When Chow telephoned Bruce in the U.S. and asked him his opinion of Mandarin films, Bruce replied, "Tell me, is this the best you can do?" Raymond liked Bruce's straightforwardness, and he dispatched the wife of his top director Lo Wei, a tough businesswoman named Liu Liang Hwa, to make Bruce an offer.

The terms of the agreement were simple. In return for his appearing in two films for Golden Harvest, Bruce was to receive US$7,500 per film. The total compensation of US$15,000 was to be paid to Bruce in monthly increments of around US$4,000, which Golden Harvest would enter into its ledgers as a "family living allotment." In addition, the subject of a bonus, which was boilerplate in most

Hollywood contracts, was raised and loosely negotiated.

There was one major problem, however, that soon reared its ugly head. Since September, Bruce had become a frequent visitor to the office of Dr. Herbert Tanney, and now the two men would be parting company for a month, maybe longer. In the event that Bruce found himself in pain,

Raymond Chow of Golden Harvest productions

Golden Harvest studio

there was no way to get his injections of cortisone. Just before Bruce's departure, Dr. Tanney prescribed to Bruce the highly addictive painkiller Darvon Compound 65.

And so on July 12, 1971, having bid farewell to his wife and two children (daughter Shannon had been born in April 1969), Lee boarded a plane to Northern Thailand and arrived in the small village of Pak Chong the following day.

Contrary to Hollywood standards, the working conditions Bruce encountered in Thailand, and subsequently endured, during the filming of The Big Boss were utterly deplorable. To begin with, the film's skeletal budget had no allowance for an actual script, and so the idea was to make up the story and dialogue as they went along. As to sets, the company filmed in and around the village's filthy whorehouses where scads of prostitutes, who were often employed as extras, plied their trade for seventy-five cents a customer.

There was also the problem of mosquitoes that flew in twenty-four hour formation with an assortment of other flying insects in search of anything that remotely resembled either food or flesh. As to ground troops, there were the cockroaches and lizards that, either singularly or in squads, feared neither man, beast, flying newspaper, nor stomping thong. Under his feet Bruce could often hear the crunch of bugs, some as large and hard as jawbreakers.

Soon Bruce was plagued with physical ailments. His voice grew hoarse from yelling. While washing a glass, he severely cut his hand, which required ten stitches. He sprained his ankle, and he was beset with flu aches and pains and fever set it.

There were personality clashes from day one, most notably between Bruce and the director, Lo Wei, who was old enough to be Bruce's grandfather and looked like an Asian version of the Pillsbury Doughboy. Lo Wei had been an actor in Mandarin films for many years and had directed eighty films for Run Run Shaw before Raymond Chow had lured him away. Within days of meeting Lo, Bruce described him as a "fame lover" and a "so-so one with an almost unbearably air of superiority." Coming from Bruce, the character analysis was laughable.

Regarding the basic accommodations, Bruce wrote to Linda complaining of horrible food shortages. "The food is terrible. This village has no beef and very little chicken, and I'm glad I brought my vitamins."

It was during this time that Bruce began losing weight. Besides his star's unexplained weight loss, director Lo Wei was becoming concerned with Bruce's indiscriminate drug use, publicly stating that Bruce was always using other people's medicine, which included injections.

While shooting in the remote village of Pak Chong, the pilot episode of Longstreet, which Stirling Silliphant had written to showcase Bruce, aired in the United States and was a sensation. As a result, Paramount wired Bruce in Pak Chong that they wanted him for three additional episodes. They offered $1,000 per episode, and Bruce countered with $2,000 per episode and got it. Apart from Paramount, several obscure independent producers approached Bruce with offers more reasonable than before, although still unacceptable. Higher up on the scale, Run Run Shaw also resurfaced, this time offering Bruce HK$250,000 (US$30,000) per film. When Bruce respectfully declined, Shaw allegedly responded by sending him a blank contract and check.

In the closing days of The Big Boss, Raymond Chow and Bruce Lee finally met when Chow flew to Pak Chong to personally shake the hand of the man who boldly stated, "I am going to be the biggest Chinese star in the world." Little did Chow know at the time that this man could have added: "And in so doing, I am going to make you a multimillionaire and the undisputed czar of what will one day be the most powerful film studio in the Far East."

With the principal photography of The Big Boss completed, in September 1971 Bruce returned to the United States where, as a matter of medical record and within days of his return, he drove to the office of Dr. Herbert Tanney for renewed injections of cortisone and a refill of his prescription for Darvon.

Following Bruce's appearance in the three previously contracted episodes of Longstreet and before beginning principal photography of Bruce's second film Fist of Fury, Linda and the children returned with Bruce to Hong Kong, where they were mobbed at the airport by Bruce's zealous fans and a feverish press. It was here that Linda encountered her first taste of Bruce's rising stardom, which was an experience she later described as unsettling.

Within days the Lee family was installed in a 500 square foot apartment in the congested Waterloo district of Kowloon. Besides Bruce, Linda, and their two children, this tiny cracker box also became home to Wu Ngan who, as a child, had lived with the Li family on Nathan Road.

By comparison, in 1971 many welfare recipients in the U.S. were living under better conditions. The Lees had no kitchen to speak of, the most rudimentary bathroom fixtures, and no laundry facilities other than hanging the family wash out the window on bamboo poles. Worst of all, there was absolutely no relief from the sweltering heat and oppressive humidity and the tormenting clacking of the gambler's Mahjongg tiles slamming on the wooden tables at all hours of the day and night.

Shortly after their October 1971 arrival in Hong Kong, Bruce and Linda attended a midnight premiere of The Big Boss. At the end of the film, following a seemingly endless period of silence, the audience suddenly jumped to their feet screaming, "Where's Bruce! Where's Bruce!" This was truly extraordinary, and amid the utter hysteria Bruce and Linda were rushed from the theater to an awaiting car.

Compared to Bruce's previous television work in the United States, The Big Boss was unquestionably substandard quality. To Chinese audiences, however, the film's thin plot, ludicrous sound effects, and poorly synchronized dubbing were irrelevant. What mattered was what rocketed this picture into an overnight smash sensation—Bruce Lee's unparalleled fighting prowess—all eight minutes of it!

Above, the gates, and below, the house of Bruce's Kowloon home

Chapter Four

The Big Boss gross receipts easily surpassed the previous records held by Gone with the Wind, The Sound of Music, and The Godfather, reportedly taking in nearly HK$4,000,000 (US$85,000) in just nineteen days. After that, it went on to break all records throughout the Mandarin Circuit and in cities as far off as Rome, Beirut and Buenos Aires.

Bruce's second picture for Golden Harvest, Fist of Fury, was filmed almost entirely on the studio's back lot. Technically, and creatively, by Hollywood standards it was of the same sub-standard quality as its predecessor. Unlike The Big Boss, Fist of Fury had a racial undercurrent that pitted the Chinese against the Japanese in their ageless and bitter blood feud and was anything but subtle.

Within minutes of the opening credits, an effeminate Japanese villain says to a gathering of Chinese: "The Chinese are a race of weaklings, no comparison to us Japanese. Just look at yourselves. You're pathetic, you know that?" Bruce soon arrives before a group of Japanese karate students. "Whenever you're ready, I'll take on any Japanese here!" Later, an Indian guard standing at a park entrance chides Bruce, "You're the wrong color, so beat it!" And near the end, a Japanese sneers at a Chinese and remarks, "If you really want to go out the door, do so like a real Chinese, on your hands and knees!" Not long after that, all hell breaks loose, and heads begin to roll.

Critical to the unfolding of Bruce's life story is a man named Bobby Baker. Originally out of Stockton, California, Baker was cast as the Russian heavy in Fist of Fury. Prior to Baker's appearance in Lee's second film it would appear from all accounts that the two men were practically strangers. None of Bruce's friends and students ever heard of

Baker, and unlike appearances in Bruce's subsequent films by known martial arts champions like Chuck Norris and Bob Wall, prior to his appearance in Fist of Fury, Baker was relatively unknown to the martial arts community. . . . .

The truth is that Lee's employment of Baker had nothing to do with Baker's acting ability or his martial arts skills. Although Baker did not appear in any of Bruce's three subsequent films, according to Linda Lee, right up to the time of her husband's death, Baker was the man responsible for bringing assorted drug contraband into Hong Kong to support Bruce's habits. Curiously Baker was in Hong Kong in late July 1973 on the evening Bruce Lee died.

Bobby Baker, a relative unknown, was cast in Fist of Fury

When it was finally released, Fist of Fury reportedly obliterated all box-office records previously set by The Big Boss, grossing nearly a million U.S. dollars in Hong Kong alone. On opening night in Singapore, hundreds

Drug paraphernalia

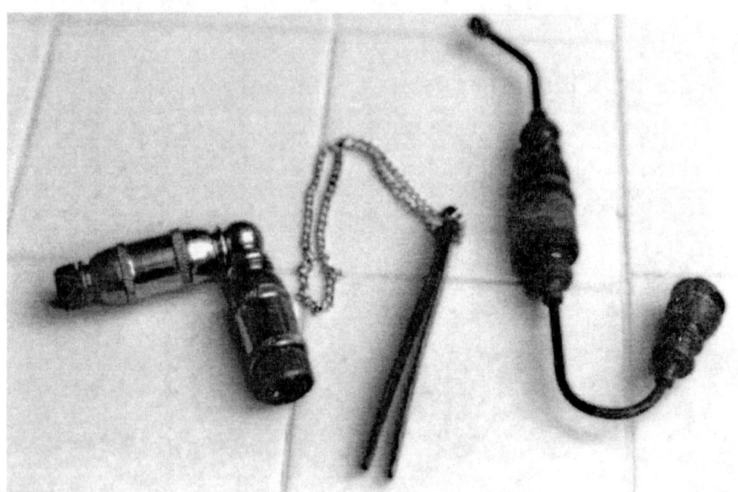

of Bruce's fans rushing to the theater triggered such a traffic gridlock that the authorities ordered the show be suspended until they could resolve the problem. In the Philippines the film ran over six months, and the government finally placed a restriction on foreign imports to protect their own domestic producers. Ironically, although Bruce had for years lashed out against what he perceived as racial prejudice in the Hollywood film industry, in the Mandarin film industry racial prejudice was netting him big dollars.

Unquestionably, with just two full-length feature films to his credit, Bruce had become the hottest show business property in the Far East. At best, it was a hollow victory. Bruce was never interested in being crowned king of the Mandarin film industry. What he desperately craved was to be a Hollywood star like Coburn and McQueen, not the star of some chop-suey version of the spaghetti western.

Although Hollywood's power structure was made aware of Bruce's success throughout the Far East, few in Hollywood were all that impressed. It wasn't long before the dragon again began to fume.

Although initially Bruce had been viewed by the press as the Far East "Golden Boy," this image ended abruptly when he one evening roughed up a reporter while yelling, "You've got thousands of shots!" With other reporters he frequently exploded because they insisted on spelling his name "Li" no matter how often he told them it should be the Americanized "Lee." There were far more startling displays of Bruce's wide and unpredictable mood swings.

On Hong Kong television Bruce viciously punched a man in the face for no reason other than to illustrate a particular element of his theory of fighting. Whatever it was Bruce was trying to prove, to the viewing public the incident came off as a blatantly ugly and unnecessary act of violence, and the press immediately took him to task.

Around this time, Bruce read an article in the China Star that described how fifteen years earlier a fellow student of Wing Chun had witnessed Bruce getting knocked down in class. Although the article was entirely true, Bruce's invincible reputation was threatened. After tracking down the writer of the article and demanding a retraction, which was not forthcoming, Bruce retaliated by suing the newspaper.

Closer to his own public, Bruce was becoming increasingly belligerent. Often when someone in the street didn't recognize him, he would turn his head, thrust out his hand and declare, "Bruce Lee—movie star!" It was boring and pompous behavior like this that was beginning to earn Bruce many enemies in Hong Kong and elsewhere.

Bruce's greatest annoyance around this time was his arch-enemy Lo Wei, and a day hardly passed that the two weren't sniveling about something having to do with the other. Invariably the matter centered on Bruce's relentless criticism of Lo's directing ability. Although Bruce had since begun avoiding the news media, Lo Wei had no such aversion, and he often babbled his side to reporters. "I do not have time to shoot loosely. I cannot tolerate. Lee's face show he is very displeased. I saw that. I said, 'I know you are "red" (hot or popular) and I cannot say I made you so. It is your own ability. But even if you are red, I have my pride.' I do not tolerate." Tolerate or not, Bruce Lee had finally had enough, and he stormed into Raymond Chow's office and told him he refused to work with Lo, announcing with great finality, "No way, Lo Wei!"

After severing his working relationship with Lo Wei, Bruce, in much the same fashion as he had earlier lashed out against the martial arts community, soon began hurling sweeping criticisms at the Mandarin filmmakers. In an interview with the Hong Kong Standard he criticized the entire Hong Kong film industry and everyone connected to it: "I'm dissatisfied with the expression of the cinematic art here in Hong Kong. It's time somebody did something about the films here. There are simply not enough soulful characters here who are committed, dedicated, and are at the same time professionals." Pausing just long enough to catch his breath, he then berated his own viewing public, who he portrayed as being dumb and naive: "The audience needs to be educated, and the one to educate them has to be somebody who is responsible. We are dealing with the masses and we have to educate them step by step. We can't do it overnight. That's what I'm doing right now. Besides, I can't even express myself fully on film here, or the audience wouldn't understand what I am talking about half the time."

Statements like this caused kenpo grandmaster Ed Parker to remark: "When Bruce ridiculed people he wasn't very tactful. He didn't pull his punches at all. You don't make friends by telling people their way of doing things is full of shit." Keenly aware that the press was becoming increasingly offended by his haughty arrogance, Lee bellowed: "Whether I succeed or not remains to be seen!"

It wasn't going to be that easy, and the writing was already on the wall. Just two weeks earlier Bruce had told Fighting Stars Magazine: "I had a heck of a problem after my second movie became a smash. I had people stop by at my door and just pass me a check for $200,000. When I asked them what it was for, they replied, 'Don't worry about it, it's just a gift to you.' I didn't even know these people. They were strangers to me."

These individuals to whom Bruce referred were neither producers nor strangers. They were members of organized crime. Triads. In the early 1970s the Sun Yee On triad exercised significant control over many movie production companies because, among other factors, their members were either heavy investors or, as shareholders in public companies, held controlling interest.

CHAPTER 5

The Way of the Dragon

If I should change my mind and deny my membership of the Hung family, I will be killed by myriads of swords.

• Triad Oath #13

In a recent edition of the South China Morning Post, the feature article, headlined "CHARTING THE TRIAD COURSE," read: "The latest blow in the fight against Hong Kong's entertainment industry crime wave has been struck, all the way from Washington, when Senate investigators last week presented a chart to a Senate Committee hearing describing the influence of organized crime on the Asian entertainment industry."

Identifying a group of twenty-eight key figures as triads, including senior members of the Sun Yee On, Wo Hop TO, 14K, and Wah Ching triads, among others, the chart graphically illustrated the main links among Asian organized crime figures who allegedly control Chinese enter tainers and their connections to the United States and other countries.

In another edition of the South China Morning Post, the following appeared under the heading of "WOUNDING CHARGE": "A car salesman accused of assaulting a film producer, who was later shot in the head at Baptist Hospital, had his case transferred to the District court yesterday. Chan Yiu-hing, 31, had his charge amended from common assault to wounding film producer Wong Long-wai and Mr. Wong Kam-chung. Mr. Wong died a few days after he was shot in his hospital bed. Chan was further charged with claiming to be a member of the Sun Yee On triad society yesterday. Magistrate Mr. Ronald Cheung extended the defendant's bail of $20,000 and ordered the defendant not to interfere with prosecution witnesses."

Because Asian gangsters have always wielded so much control in the Hong Kong film industry, Bruce Lee faced obstacles far more complex—and potentially lethal—than any he faced in Hollywood. Still today, in addition to grotesque beatings, actors are kidnapped and actresses raped for refusing to cooperate with triads. Knife slashings are commonplace, limbs are severed, agents are assassinated, and fire-bombings are not infrequent. Following a recent horrific incident in which five masked armed men with pistols and knives burst into the Mandarin Films studio and made off with the negatives to a film that was soon scheduled for release, the film community had finally had enough. Five days following the Mandarin Films robbery, waves of actors, directors, screenwriters, cameramen and production crew members marched on Police Headquarters in the business district of Hong Kong. The protesters carried a large banner that read "Show Business Against Violence," and demanded that the police do something to protect the movie community from extortion.

Back in the early 1970s when Bruce was first employed by Golden Harvest Studios, besides controlling the stuntmen and extras routinely hired by Hong Kong film producers, triad kingpins commonly demanded prominent Hong Kong entertainers enter into lucrative management contracts. In return for a percentage of the client's income, triads controlled the careers of movie stars, producers, pop singers, and the like. Moreover, an individual who was both a triad and a film producer was not at all unusual. As with the Italian Mafia, little has changed over the past two decades.

Typically, triad influence begins early in the star's career. Often the individual is given a substantial sum of cash as a gift. With others it may be clothing, drugs, or a flashy new sports car. Whatever the hook, the point is the foot gets in the door, and when the star finally shines bright, the entire body follows and the door slams in its wake. Forever.

The problem with Bruce Lee was that his star rose too fast. And by the time anyone noticed that he was breaking box-office records throughout Asia, he was already talking about how he planned on using his good fortune in the east as a stepping stone back to the west. Unfortunately for Bruce, the triads were only interested in his stepping into their office to sign a management contract.

Bruce stiffened with defiance. This was an outrage. He wasn't some chump from Movie Town. He was an American and a dues paying member of the prestigious Screen Actors Guild. And besides, he hadn't made much money on these films, just ask Raymond Chow. A meager fifteen grand was all Golden Harvest had paid Lee. For two pictures. Not that it was any of their damn business.

All right. That was the past. What about the future? What about it? Well, who was to protect Lee from all the potential hazards and nefarious deeds and misdeeds known to occur to Hong Kong entertainers not under contract? What! Bruce was the King of Kung fu, or hadn't they heard? Well, perhaps it might be better understood if the problem was presented in the form of a question. Did Bruce intend to make more films with Golden Harvest in Asia?

True to his nature, Bruce's answer was swift in coming, and in early 1972 he severed his relationship, implied or otherwise, with Golden Harvest Studios and formed Concord Productions with Raymond Chow. Clean slate. As to any contracts with the triads, management or otherwise, if Raymond or anyone else was willing to pay tea money to the triads, that was their business. Not that this was unfamiliar territory to Bruce. He'd lived it as a street gang member. He'd worked in films with his father and so he knew this was standard operating procedure throughout much of the Mandarin film industry. The problem was that Bruce no longer identified with being a street gang member. Hollywood had given him a new image and, even if he had to shout it from the top of Victoria Peak, no one was going to cheapen his career by tying him to organized crime.

After forming Concord Productions, Bruce wrote his first and only script, which he called The Way of the Dragon. Besides taking a sole screenwriting credit, he cast himself in the starring role and used the picture as his directorial debut. According to Linda Lee, Bruce made this decision to do everything himself because he simply had no confidence in anyone in Hong Kong. Although this may have been partly true, one cannot ignore the strong possibility that in light of Concord Productions being a newly formed film company with no affiliation with the triads, Bruce surely would have had some degree of difficulty getting people to work for him.

Once the script was completed, Bruce faced yet another major obstacle. As a renegade production, The Way of the Dragon could not be shot in triad-controlled Southeast Asia. To circumvent the problem, Bruce took a skeletal film crew 6,000 miles away to Rome where they shot the picture in the summer of 1972. It was yet another big gamble. Historically this was the first Hong Kong production ever shot in Europe. The film co-starred Chuck Norris in his first role and Nora Miao, a young and beautiful Chinese actress who soon joined the list of starlets alleged to be romantically involved with Bruce.

When The Way of the Dragon was released, critics, with few exceptions, viewed the picture as a foolish, self-indulgent, routine film of home movie quality. Essentially the film's tiresome plot amounted to a group of Italian mafioso villains trying to force an innocent and naive Chinese family to sign over the deed to their restaurant. The end product was two hours of episodic violence (5% of the film's $100,000 budget went to buy gallons of artificial blood) fueled by more racial slurs aimed at Japanese-bashing. Aside from the ending fight sequences between Bruce and Chuck Norris, the film had little redeeming value.

Prior to the release of The Way of the Dragon, Bruce had boasted to the press that the film's box-office would eclipse his two previous movies, further predicting that the picture would gross HK$5,000,000 (US$1,060,000) in Hong Kong alone. When the film was released in early 1973, the

Chapter Five

Nora Miao co-starred in The Way of the Dragon

gross receipts fell far short of Bruce's bold predictions, netting a measly US$179,000 profit throughout all of Southeast Asia in 1973. Rather than concede that the film had been a financial disaster, Bruce and Raymond reported to the press that the film's grosses had surpassed Lee's earlier predictions. Bruce's self-imposed power play had failed miserably. He had made a premature attempt to return to Hollywood before things had become too hot on the Mandarin film circuit, yet, aside from his unparalleled physical prowess, he was not on a par with stars like Coburn and McQueen. In the west, critics attacked Lee's violence.

Unfortunately, Bruce was again down to bedrock. As to the luxuriant purchases he had been making, which also included a new Mercedes and a complete new wardrobe of Italian suits and shoes, these had been made possible through funds advanced to him by Raymond Chow on the strength of the anticipated profits from The Way of the Dragon.

According to legend, for centuries the area of Kowloon Tong has been the home of nine dragons and has a horrible reputation of being a destroyer of rich families. Within days of taking up residence in Kowloon Tong, one by one the entire family fell ill. Fearing the house had become plagued with bad fortune (Feng Shui), Bruce summoned a mystic fortune teller, who arrived carrying a large device that resembled a box compass with its magnetic needle free to fall upon any of the twelve signs of the Chinese zodiac.

Upon examining the premises, the fortuneteller became gravely concerned. The entire place had bad Feng Shui. Far worse than the fact that the house sat directly beneath the flight approach to the Kai Tak Airport and was facing in the wrong direction, nowhere was there any har

Park in Kowloon

mony between spiritual and material things. Because of grave warnings of the fortuneteller, Bruce had installed on his roof a pat-kwa, which is a small mirror set in an octagonal wooden frame, whose function it is to reflect away bad fortune.

According to the Chinese elders, when Bruce took up residence in the suburb, it caused anger and rivalry among the mythical dragon beasts. Mel Tobias, Hong Kong film critic said, "You know that Bruce Lee, in Chinese, means 'little dragon,' right? And that house he lived in Kowloon Tong had something to do with dragons. And you know that the Chinese are very superstitious. Well, this whole thing out there in Kowloon Tong smacks of bad Feng Shui!"

There were other problems. During this time, Bruce

continued grappling with reporters, who now began snooping around his private life, particularly his alleged romantic liaisons. Who was he sleeping with, they demanded? Surely he wasn't faithful to this pale gwie-lo (foreign devil) girl. What was he hiding and where?

It wasn't long before the press hounds focused in on Betty Ting-pei (Tong Mei-lai), a C-rated Taiwanese actress who had a sordid reputation in the scandal press and was associated with indiscriminate drug use and free love. Although Bruce and Linda first met Betty Ting coming down the driveway of the Regency House in Kowloon, it has been rumored that the beautiful temptress had been purposely planted in Bruce's life by a particular triad crime syndicate.

Despite how the two met, the press thought it far too coincidental that this curvaceous dragon lady, who had not been employed by Concord Productions in any capacity, had conveniently surfaced with The Way of the Dragon film company 6,000 miles away in Rome. Within days, Bruce was quoted in the press as having told Linda that Betty was "the one shining light on an otherwise dull film set," further saying that "Betty quite makes my day. She's a revelation with her cleverness." It wasn't likely Linda saw anything clever about the woman at all. Among other things, Betty drew an uncanny resemblance to Bruce's college heartthrob Amy Sanbo.

Not long after Bruce had met Betty, a reporter cornered Linda at a function she was attending without her husband. "It is said that Bruce is very close to certain actresses," the reporter blurted out loudly. "How do you feel about it?" Reportedly Linda was momentarily stunned, then responded, "That is his matter." Although distasteful to Linda and

Chapter Five

Betty Ting-pei

in direct conflict with her religious upbringing, it was the proper response. To successful Chinese men, concubines are as much a status symbol as a Rolls Royce. It is simply part of the image. Although outlawed in Hong Kong only since 1970, concubinage (a form of polygamy) is more akin to what the western world calls mistresses. These stables of women give new meaning to the phrase "drop dead good looks" and are still publicly displayed throughout Hong Kong.

Although The Way of the Dragon failed to attract a reputable international distributor, when Raymond Chow announced that the picture had grossed over HK$5,000,000 in Hong Kong alone, independent producers from around the world again began to take notice.

Run Run Shaw was hardly a dead issue, and a day failed to pass that the press neglected to ask about Lee's relationship with the Shaw Brothers. A reporter arrived at the studio for an interview and asked if Bruce would work for Run Run. "If I have a good script, I will consider it," Bruce replied. "I want to be neutral and act for whichever company can provide me with good scripts. I don't want to be involved in any conflicts or competition here."

An interesting set of comments. Right from the dragon's fiery mouth the implication that he is not contractually obligated to Raymond Chow, despite their partnership in Concord Productions. This to be followed by the statement that he has no desire to get involved in political disputes. Within minutes there are six reporters on the scene, all pressing the same issue. Aggravated, Bruce snaps, "Tell them I've signed for twenty films with the Shaws!" As Amy Sanbo had years earlier so adeptly perceived, Bruce at times seemed to gain pleasure from stirring up trouble.

The turmoil in Bruce's life had also begun to turn inward. "It's like I'm in jail!" Bruce complained. "I am like the monkey in the zoo!"

It seemed to Bruce that everyone was out to get him, especially the endless wave of greedy, insincere producers. "They think I am only interested in money," he protested. "That's why they all try to lure me onto their sets by promising me huge sums of nothing else." Apparently Bruce had forgotten that he had earlier written in his Chief Personal Aim how he would first acquire $10,000,000 and then live a life of peace and harmony. Perhaps these film producers traveled a similar path toward enlightenment.

Noteworthy to many biographers is that around this time Bruce and Raymond Chow were increasingly at odds. When a Golden Harvest fan magazine, which was published by Chow, ran a feature article suggesting that Chow was the brains behind Concord Productions, Bruce exploded: "The article puts forth a notion that I am a brainless child who relies solely on Raymond! But I am not... in stead I am my own boss, and I have as much brains as others!"

Besides becoming paranoid about his business associate, one by one Bruce became testy with his personal friends. Arriving at Kai Tak Airport, Dan Inosanto, Bruce's top student who had traveled to Hong Kong to informally film a fight sequence with Lee, nonchalantly commented to Bruce that he looked thin. Without warning, Bruce violently punched Inosanto, slamming him against a wall. Inosanto stood motionless, staring back at Bruce, who angrily proclaimed that he was "as strong as ever!"

Although according to Inosanto Bruce's power was actually greater than before, what concerned him was Bruce's alarming weight loss. Inosanto wasn't the only one troubled over Bruce's health. Many of those around him had begun to comment that he looked ill.

In November 1972 Bruce consulted with Hong Kong physician Dr. Otto Y.T. Au. Bruce's chief complaints: (1) sunken cheeks, (2) profuse sweating, (3) severe acne, and (4) weight loss. Upon examining Lee, Dr. Au described him as a slender Chinese male weighing 124 pounds and diagnosed him as having axially hyperdrosis (profuse sweating).

Following Dr. Au's diagnosis, Bruce was admitted to Canossa Hospital where Au surgically removed the sweat glands under Bruce's arms, after which he advised Bruce to begin eating a balanced and proper diet and prescribed medication for acute anxiety. Tragically, thirty-four years ago, due to the scarcity of scientific information on the subject, Dr. Au failed to associate Bruce's complaints to his use of anabolic steroids.

As early as 1968, martial arts legend Joe Lewis, who at six feet in height and 200 pounds of solid muscle literally towered over Bruce, stated publicly: "Bruce was real self-conscious about his narrow chest. He had a flat ribcage and his legs were really skinny and that really bothered him. He wanted some meat on his body. He was 5-foot-7 and weighted about 138 at that time, and he had been lifting for awhile. He was really strong, but he just had no muscle mass."

Besides having a great fear of being hit by someone much bigger than he, Bruce inevitably became obsessed with his onscreen body image. Essentially what he desired was a highly defined musculature (referred to by bodybuilders as "ripped"), and in order to achieve that he began taking anabolic steroids through a process known as "stacking," which is a complex method of mixing various steroids and is often upsetting to the user's stomach. To combat the problem of bloating, which results from excessive water retention brought on by one's use of steroids, Bruce was a frequent user of diuretics. Although this greatly reduced the excessive water content in his muscles, and thus gave him the desired "ripped" appearance, it was a dangerous practice that frequently placed him in a life-threatening state of dehydration.

In addition to dramatically increasing muscle size while simultaneously reducing body fat levels, steroids greatly enhance an athlete's speed, power and endurance, and temporarily intensify the male sex drive. Although Bruce had initially taken steroids to enhance his musculature, he was surprised when the drug activated his sexuality which, owing to his cryptorchidism, had to this point been an insignificant element of his life.

The psychological profile noted in users of anabolic steroids aptly describes Bruce Lee in the early 1970s and includes: (1) an increase in self-esteem, sometimes to the point of severe narcissism and self-obsession, (2) an increased physical drive to exercise intensely, (3) a decrease in the user's ability to accept poor performance or failure, and (4) a marked decrease in their tolerance of others.

Viewed in its historical context, it is important to note that at the time Bruce began using anabolic steroids, the life-threatening side effects of steroid use were not known and, consequently, the use of these synthetic hormones by amateur, Olympic, and professional athletes (including other martial artists) was not illegal or uncommon. Nevertheless, this does not allay the fact that Bruce had begun taking what current scientific research has proven to be one of the most physically damaging and psychologically debilitating of all drugs.

Anabolic steroids became the solution to Bruce Lee's

main problems in life, at least for a while. Jim Stalworth, a junior at Rawlings High School in Kearney, Nebraska, talked publicly about his own first impressions of the drug, which would have been most alluring to Bruce: "Anabolic steroids do not put you in a stupor or in a hallucinogenic state, but they give you an up, all-around bad-ass mentality that far exceeds that of either normal life or any other narcotic I've ever tried." The operative words, which inevitably became Bruce Lee's calling card, are "bad-ass mentality."

Dr. Au remedied three minor complaints of steroid users, those of profuse sweating, acute anxiety, and acne. However, athletes and bodybuilders who continue to take steroids over a long time run the risk of severely damaging their heart, kidneys and liver. To avert these physical ailments, it is imperative that the user periodically discontinues taking steroids, the rule of thumb being an equal time on and off, i.e., fourteen days on, fourteen off; thirty days on, thirty off, etcetera.

Even for a short time, withdrawal from anabolic steroids is the opposing side of the double-edged sword. Commonly reported side effects include acute anxiety, insomnia, lack of energy, depression, mania, impotence, feelings of inferiority, loss of muscle mass, and thoughts of suicide. Not uncommon is the individual's need for a sedative, often in the form of alcohol or other CNS depressant, to counteract these ill effects.

In retrospect it is not surprising that in October 1972, Bruce began to exhibit signs of physical and psychological deterioration. Symptomatic of his increasing and unchecked use of anabolic steroids, he had long since fallen pray to severe mood swings, which were frequently coupled with unpredictable outbursts of what today are commonly known to steroid users as "roid rages."

Aside from the matter of Bruce needing a period of downtime while he temporarily discontinued his use of steroids, following the release of The Way of the Dragon there was another reason for this noticeable lull in Bruce's career. The problem was that The Way of the Dragon had shown that Chinese kung fu movies backdropped against a European setting were destined for box-office failure. This meant that Bruce was forced to return to filming in Southeast Asia where Concord Productions had no working agreement with the triad hierarchy.

It was during this period of several months, while unknown participants were allegedly conducting negotiations with the triads, that Bruce filmed isolated fight sequences with Laker basketball star Kareem Abdul-Jabbar, hapkido master Ji Hand Jai, and martial arts protégé Dan Inosanto. Primarily, Bruce planned to submit this footage to Hollywood producers in the hope of bolstering interest. Although technically this footage was filmed in triad-controlled Hong Kong, Bruce shot the footage informally, without a script, passing the matter off as a glorified version of home movies. As he had done earlier in filming The Way of the Dragon, it would appear that Bruce was again hedging accepted policy.

Although Bruce and Concord Productions clearly had their problems in Hong Kong, 7,000 miles away in the United States, producer Fred Weintraub had not given up on Bruce. Having landed a position as creative vice president at Warner Brothers in 1969, where he had overseen the creation of Woodstock and Rage, Weintraub formed a production company called Sequoia Pictures with Paul Heller, who had helped create Dirty Harry with Clint Eastwood and

Skin Game with James Garner.

While Bruce was in Hong Kong making his first two films for Golden Harvest, Weintraub kept the door open by offering to screen, upon their completion, the two finished products for Warner executives. Upon viewing The Big Boss and Fist of Fury, however, the executives simply passed. Undeterred, Weintraub and Heller commissioned unknown screenwriter Michael Allin to deliver a first draft screenplay to what would later be called Enter the Dragon.

Their timing could not have been better. Based on Bruce's success at bringing together Asian and Caucasian martial arts stars in The Way of the Dragon, coupled with President Nixon's historic trip to Mainland China and Sequoia's show of good faith in financing Allin's script, Warner Brothers agreed to finance the picture. The problem now, however, was getting Raymond Chow to agree to the terms.

According to Robert Clouse's book Bruce Lee: the Biography, Fred Weintraub flew to Hong Kong to set the final deal with Raymond. After two weeks of negotiations Weintraub could not get Raymond Chow to sign on the dotted line. Although Chow kept stating that he thought it was a bad move for Bruce, everyone knew it was a potential nightmare for Golden Harvest, as they might ultimately lose control of their one and only star. Although Bruce seemed to favor making the deal, Weintraub could never get Bruce and Raymond in the same room at the same time.

Finally on the night before departing Hong Kong, Weintraub found himself seated with the two men at a prearranged dinner party. Deciding to give it a final shot, Weintraub told Bruce that it was a shame that, without this deal (or one like it), he probably would never be an interna tional star. Perhaps Raymond was right and Bruce should play it safe and focus on the Mandarin film industry. Bruce seemed to want to make the deal and couldn't understand the problem. Weintraub recalled what happened next. "With Raymond sitting nearby, I told Bruce I couldn't make a deal with Raymond, anyway. Bruce looked at me, then at his wife Linda, and finally at Raymond. 'Make the deal.' Raymond smiled and said, 'I think it's a wonderful idea.'" Of course, apart from the problem of losing control of Bruce, a three-legged deal involving a studio as powerful as Warner Brothers could result in Golden Harvest, along with Chow and any silent partners he may have had, losing its exclusive control of the purse strings.

Having agreed to the deal in principle, Bruce Lee and Raymond Chow flew to Los Angeles where, as Concord Productions, they executed the contracts with Warner Brothers and Sequoia Pictures. As the ink was drying on the pages, Bruce and producer Weintraub drove to the home of the screenwriter Michael Allin to discuss the script.

Allin recently recalled the meeting as if it were yesterday, as he gazed out over the Atlantic shoreline from his home in East Hampton. "I was a little uncomfortable meeting Bruce Lee. I had seen his previous films and, frankly, I thought I was about to meet some direct descendent of Buddha. I guess I had this vision of Bruce in the long robes, meditating before the meeting, tea and a lot of wise old proverbs. Anyway, in walks Bruce, and the first thing he does is open his leather handbag and whips out this color brochure of a Rolls Royce. He practically throws it at me and says, 'This sucker just ordered, Rolls Royce!' I didn't know what to say. I was embarrassed. Finally I had to say something because it was obvious that he was waiting for my response, so I said, 'What color?' Bruce seemed to pounce on the question, 'The only color there is—gold!'"

Following the initial awkward moment, the group got down to discussing Allin's script. According to Allin, there was only one speed bump to get over, which was Bruce's height. While Allin got busy on rewrites, Bruce returned to the Beverly Wilshire Hotel where he eagerly placed a call to Steve McQueen.

Two years had passed since Bruce shook his fist at McQueen's house while proclaiming that he would one day be a bigger and brighter star. Bruce told McQueen that he was back from Hong Kong and then began to gloat about how his movies were doing big business and how he had just signed to do a picture with Warner Brothers. McQueen waited until Bruce had finally finished, then said, "That's great, Bruce." The next day Bruce received by personal messenger an enormous picture of McQueen, which was in the form of the standard one-sheet used by studios to advertise their films. The life-sized glossy photograph of McQueen was personally autographed by the superstar: "To Bruce Lee, my greatest fan. Steve McQueen." Bruce was so furious that he had the one-sheet mounted on a huge section of cardboard and set it up for a workout, then blasted the images to pieces in a martial arts frenzy.

CHAPTER 6

Enter the Dragon

Although Bruce had finally been granted his impassioned wish to star in a feature-length motion picture produced by a major U.S. film company, it did little to satisfy his insatiable ego and there was trouble from the very start.

In January 1973, Hollywood producers Fred Weintraub and Paul Heller arrived in Hong Kong with their Hollywood director Bob Clouse and a contingent of Hollywood actors. Clearly this was not the motley bunch of gross incompetents from the Hong Kong film industry whom Bruce had vehemently criticized for the past two years. Hollywood had come to the Far East with Warner Brothers' money, and to many of the key players in the Hollywood contingent, Bruce Lee was a Mandarin star, not a Hollywood star, and Bruce didn't like it.

When Bruce first met Bob Clouse, he walked up to him and tapped on his own cheek. "Never forget," Bruce grinned amusingly.

"Forget what?" the director asked.

"This is my bad side!" Bruce replied.

Recalled Michael Allin, "From that point forward Clouse thought Bruce was a real jerk, and he often spoke very contemptuously of him."

What soon took on the appearance of a circus sideshow became even more farcical when Michael Allin arrived in Hong Kong in the first week in January 1973. There really wasn't any reason for Allin to be there, but the producers, due to the fact that Allin had not been paid much for his work, had thrown in a free trip to Hong Kong as part of the deal.

Upon his arrival, Allin came across a newspaper headline written in Chinese and featuring a picture of himself. Believing that the article was a publicity blurb about the screenwriter's arrival in Hong Kong, he politely asked a Chinese woman he had befriended in the airport to translate. Although Allin had not spoken or seen Bruce since their initial meeting in Los Angeles nearly three months earlier, he was utterly flabbergasted to learn that the article said that Bruce, furious with Allin, had ordered the producers to boot the screenwriter out of Hong Kong! After calming the befuddled scriptwriter, the woman assured him that the article was typical of the tabloid hyperbole that frequently surrounded Bruce Lee, and Allin dismissed it at that.

Hours later Allin arrived in the lobby of the Hyatt Regency for what was supposed to be a pleasant dinner with Bob Clouse and Fred Weintraub. Clouse had for years worn a hearing aid in both ears and was surveying the dining room for a quiet table. Allin casually strolled up to the two men (each a borderline teetotaler), amazed to find both of them shit-faced. Clouse began yelling. "What the hell are you doing here, man! Bruce is coming!"

Weintraub picked up where Clouse left off, "What the hell did you do to Bruce! He's nuts! He walked out!"

Allin suddenly recalled the tabloid article in the air

port. "What's wrong, anyway?"

Clouse began yelling. "Everything's gone to hell! He took a swing at Linda and then locked himself in his den! Jesus Christ, man, get the hell out of here!"

Typical of Hollywood's legendary infighting and back stabbing, and to appease Bruce, either Clouse or Weintraub or someone, in Allin's absence, had handed Bruce a bunch of hack rewrites that literally put Bruce over the side. And rather than place the responsibility where it rightfully belonged, it was far easier to blame the novice screenwriter.

Regardless of the fireworks, Allin had just arrived in Hong Kong and he wasn't about to be run out of town. Besides, the trip was part of his meager compensation. Having agreed to steer clear of the volatile Bruce Lee, Allin took in the sights and sounds of Hong Kong and then returned to the United States a week later.

Over the years it has been widely reported that no sooner had the Hollywood contingent arrived in Hong Kong than Bruce proclaimed that he hated the script. Although he had read Allin's screenplay before the commencement of principal photography and had accepted the final draft, suddenly he found serious flaws in Allin's writing. Bruce's stated opinion was, "Hey, there's only one reason this movie's being made and that's because people believe that with Bruce Lee in the movie it's going to make back its negative cost. It's not being made because it's a fine piece of literature!"

Bruce's protest had nothing to do with the underlying message, prophetic or otherwise, of Allin's script, but rather particular words that Bruce had difficulty pronouncing, like the character name "Braithwaith," which Bruce, because he rolled his R's and W's, found difficult to pronounce. In his book Bruce Lee, author Jesse Glover states: "One thing that I have never heard mentioned in writing about Bruce is that he stuttered... Sometimes his voice would jam up and he wasn't able to speak... If someone laughed at him when it happened, Bruce was afraid he might explode and attack them."

Of course, the real issue Bruce faced was about humiliation, because most people attribute stuttering to fear. And for Bruce Lee, who was being heralded throughout the world as the king of kung fu, to also be viewed as a man beset with fear created a tremendous inner conflict.

Following Allin's departure from Hong Kong, Warner Brothers began sending rewritten versions of the script, hoping to placate Bruce. Twelve days later yet another script arrived from Hollywood, prompting Fred Weintraub to call the studio to tell them he was quitting. Then Linda called Weintraub and pleaded with him to stay on and to give Bruce just a little more time. Another week passed, and still no sign of Bruce. Fed up with Lee's unprofessional, childish delays, Weintraub finally threatened to fire him and have him replaced, angrily shouting, "Who needs this guy?"

Weintraub had misdiagnosed the real problem, which was essentially Bruce's escalating drug use and his inability to balance and counterbalance the effects and side effects of one chemical against another. As a result, he was in a perpetual state of emotional upheaval and instability.

Three weeks passed before Bruce managed to get things together to the point that he eventually showed up for work. Many found him to be extremely withdrawn and apprehensive. "He was nervous the day we actually started shooting," Weintraub recalled. "You could see him twitching. Bob said to me, 'He's twitching.' The first scene with him was a very simple one, but it took twenty takes."

Bruce had good reason to be nervous. From the first day there was grumbling from his countrymen about foreign devils ripping off the Chinese and commercializing their ancient art of kung fu. Although Bruce was himself three-quarters Chinese, because of his U.S. citizenship he was considered more an American and was often included in the growing anti-Americanism sentiment. The fact that he was married to a Caucasian didn't help matters.

Not long into the production, things really heated up when Bruce's martial arts teacher, Master Yip Man, unexpectedly passed away. From around the world, practitioners of Wing Chun, old friends, admirers, and representatives of most styles of Chinese martial arts, attended the funeral rites. Although it had long been rumored that Bruce harbored a grudge against his old sifu, Hong Kong was shocked and horrified when Lee, citing his busy shooting schedule, did not attend the services. The following day newspaper editorials chided him, the popular response to the incident being perfectly depicted in a widely circulated cartoon that showed Lee tugging his forelock at the shrine of Yip Man and saying "Sorry, Master, I am too busy making money to go to your funeral ceremony."

Besides the slings and arrows directed at Bruce from his own people and the undercurrent of racial hostility all too reminiscent of his childhood, the film set was crawling with triads who had been hired as extras and stuntmen, several of whom mocked Bruce and openly challenged him to fights. Moreover, in the front office, rumor had circulated that Run Run Shaw had planted informants at every level of production.

Once principal photography began, there were more problems. In an early scene, Bruce had to get past a live cobra. To everyone's horror, the snake struck at Bruce and bit him. Although the snake had been devenomized, its bite resulted in nearly a week of nagging pain. Weeks later while filming a fight sequence, Bruce received a severe laceration to his hand, which cut an artery and required a dozen stitches. Within hours of his injury, Bruce was informed that his lacerated hand had not been an accident. Soon there were death threats and counter threats, and an ugly fight erupted between Bruce and one of the triads.

In the closing weeks, Bruce pulled on every reserve. It was the

Yip Man

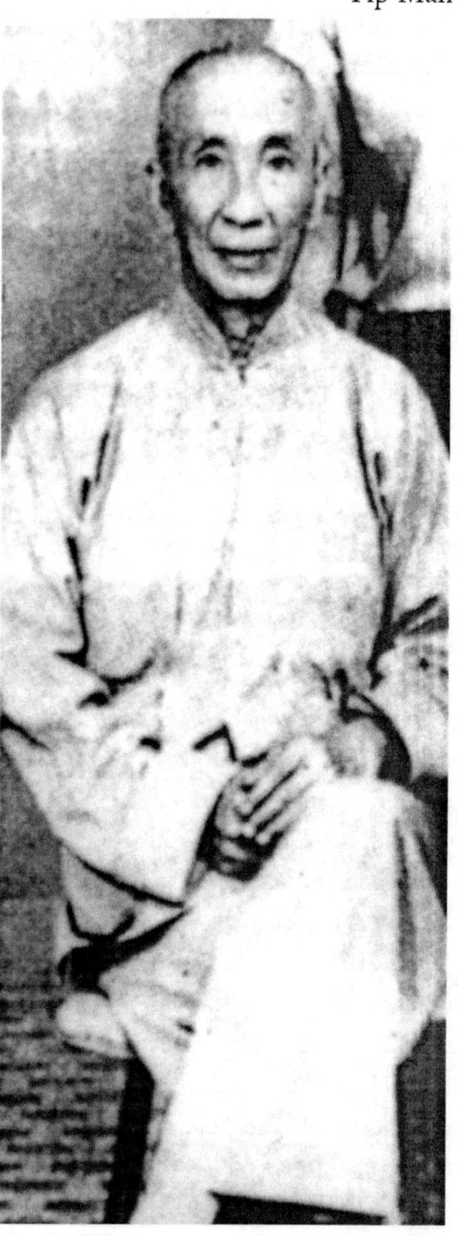

gamble of a lifetime, and the stakes were enormously high. If only he could hold up for a few more days, even hours, then he could flee to the United States and take a much-needed rest.

In the final days of shooting, Bruce again began to exhibit a wide range of physical and psychological problems. Many commented that he looked seriously ill, while others noted that he appeared to be in a perpetual daze. Maria Yi, who co-starred with Bruce in The Big Boss, stated publicly, "Near the end I found that Bruce seemed to have amnesia. While I met him in the studio, he often took out from his handbag the picture of his beloved car and asked me to comment on it. He repeated this action four or five times a day without knowing that he had done it before. I felt that he was unusual."

Apparently there were other forces who were concerned about Bruce's future, for it was around this time that a sizeable amount of life insurance began to be taken out in Bruce's name. Although there is no record of Bruce having applied for life insurance before February 1973, it was learned after his death that his life had recently been insured under three separate policies.

The first policy was through the Screen Actors Guild, of which Bruce was a member. In 1973 the policy paid a single death benefit of $5,000. No one has ever raised any question about this coverage, nor should they have.

The second policy, taken out through American International Assurance Company (AIA), which is a private limited company based in Singapore, was for US$200,000 (US$2,600,000 in 2002) and covered a period of five years from 2/1/73 to 1/31/78. The beneficiary was listed as "Linda Emery Lee if living, otherwise Brandon Bruce Lee and Shannon Emery Lee, children of the deceased, in the share of one-half each." In addition to there being some question whether Bruce was ever aware of the AIA policy, it is important to note that in April 1973 Bruce had listed on his federal income tax his total earnings at a mere $17,000.

That the AIA policy had been applied for less than six months before Bruce's death was curious enough. That a third policy (requested by Linda on April 30, 1973) through Lloyds of London for a staggering US$1,350,000 (US$17,500,000 in 2002) was issued ninety days later was patently alarming. This brought the total life insurance to over a million and a half U.S. dollars. To put this in perspective, today this would be equivalent to nearly $20,000,000 of life insurance on a man with very little equity in his house and a total cash worth just over $200,000.

The date upon which all three life insurance policies were in place was May 5, 1973.

On May 10, just five days after the issuance of the Lloyds of London insurance policy, Bruce was dubbing on a sound stage at Golden Harvest Studios when he suddenly felt nauseated. He quickly excused himself and walked to a nearby vacant restroom where he then felt extremely weak.

According to Linda Lee, Bruce later told her that to the best of his knowledge he did not lose consciousness, for he recalled pretending that he was groping around on the floor for his glasses, this in response to hearing someone enter the restroom. Nevertheless, several individuals in the dubbing room later said that Bruce had been gone for well over twenty minutes, which seemed like a considerable time to be away at a nearby restroom. Anyway, upon returning to the dubbing room, Bruce suddenly lost consciousness and collapsed to the floor where he then vomited and his body

Baptist Hospital

began convulsing.

Immediately several men ran to Raymond Chow, who was working in his office nearby, and informed him of Bruce's frightening condition. Rather than summon an ambulance, Chow called Dr. Charles Langford at Baptist Hospital and told him that Bruce had collapsed, may be choking on his own vomit, and had gone into convulsions. Dr. Langford instructed Chow to transport Bruce to Baptist at once.

Upon his arrival at Baptist Hospital, Bruce was attended to by Dr. Langford, an American, who later testified: "Lee was brought in by several men from the studio. He was suffering from high fever and was unconscious and unresponsive in the emergency room. First there were breathing noises, then they stopped. There was a series of convulsions. Three other doctors were summoned, including a neurosurgeon, Dr. Peter Woo. Lee was going through muscle contraction and relaxation. The entire body was involved in this motion, but the upper limbs gave us the most difficulty because he was very strong and was difficult to control. After the failure of Lee to respond for a period, and after waiting for the neurosurgeon to examine him, we gave him Mannitol to reduce the swelling of the brain which we had detected. It took us one and a half hours to make Lee conscious. After Lee was revived, his eyes were moving to the right and left in a circular motion and his speech was slurred." When asked if Bruce's condition could have been caused from overwork and exhaustion, Langford testified that it could not. In later testimony, the neurosurgeon, Dr. Woo, stated that a blood test suggested a possible malfunction of the kidneys, and further testified that Bruce had told him that he had taken marijuana that same day, which Dr. Woo presumed to mean that Bruce had chewed the leaf. Prior to Bruce's discharge from Baptist Hospital, Dr. Langford prescribed Valium for Bruce's anxiety. Bruce was then transferred to St. Theresa's Hospital for additional testing, at which time he was coherent.

Two weeks later Bruce traveled to the United States, and on May 25, 1973 was examined by noted Beverly Hills physician Dr. Harold L. Karpman. Since his initial collapse on May 10, Bruce had undergone a complete work-up at St. Theresa Hospital in Hong Kong and had brought the test results with him.

Apart from telling Dr. Karpman that he absolutely hated Chinese food, Bruce's major complaints were that he: (1) had been under a great deal of tension for the past several years, (2) suffered from insomnia, (3) complained of a poor appetite, and (4) had lost twenty pounds over a two-year period.

In Bruce's particular case, it is important to realize that a loss of twenty pounds of body weight over a two-year period is highly significant. Besides his overuse of diuretics, which significantly reduced his body's percentage of water, Bruce had an extremely low percentage of body fat. The result was that under these conditions a loss of over 14 percent of his body's muscular mass was noticeable in Bruce and made him appear emaciated.

Dr. Karpman ordered a complete work-up and neurological examination of Bruce, including a brain scan and brain flow study and electroencephalogram, and noted that Bruce's body was not in a state of dehydration. There was no evidence of a brain tumor, and his heart function and vessels were normal. As astonishing as it sounds, although Dr. Karpman was "embarrassed" by Bruce's weight (125 lb.), he found him to be in superb physical health. Karpman's frustration is noted by his sworn deposition on July 24, 1974, a year after Lee's death:

Q: And when was the first time you treated Mr. Lee?
A: I didn't treat him; I examined him.
Q: Did you come up with a working diagnosis?
A: Diagnosis of what?

And later, upon being reminded of Lee's use of marijuana:

Q: If you had known of [Lee's cannabis use] or if he had told you that, would it have affected your opinion as to what might have been his problem?
A: Well, you see, I really didn't understand what his problem was at that point –

Unable to arrive at a working diagnosis, Karpman referred Bruce to a neurologist, Dr. David Reisbord. Working in collaboration with a team of colleagues at UCLA Medical Center, Reisbord came up with the final impression that Bruce had a convulsive disorder, grand mal, idiopathic. In lay terms this simply said that Bruce was prone to generalized body convulsions whose cause was unknown. After prescribing the drug Dilantin, which is a commonly used medication for the management of epilepsy, Dr. Reisbord gave Bruce a clean bill of health.

Finally, during his deposition, Dr. Karpman said he was puzzled over a strange laboratory test that had been run in Hong Kong when Bruce was admitted to Baptist Hospital. The test was an elevated kidney test for blood urea nitrogen (BUN), which had concerned Dr. Woo at Baptist Hospital on May 10, but was normal on May 25 when Karpman examined Bruce in Los Angeles. Ultimately Karpman felt that the extraordinarily high test result was probably an error, that what the Hong Kong laboratory technician meant to type was 9.2 instead of 92 (normal values range from 10 to 20 mg per 100 ml of blood).

During his deposition, however, Karpman stated

there was a possibility of a kidney problem causing Bruce's convulsions. Further, considering the events of the ensuing six weeks, it seems highly unlikely that this strange test result was a typographical error, as Karpman had initially theorized.

CHAPTER 7

The Final Curtain

"When we come to that stage in our lives when we are less able to accomplish but more able to enjoy, we will have attained the wisdom that Ecclesiastes finally found after so many false starts and disappointments."

• Dr. Wayne W. Dyer

Following the extensive medical examination at UCLA, Bruce drove to Warner Brothers where he viewed a screening of Enter the Dragon in its final cut. When the house lights came up, he knew that he had finally arrived. Clenching his fists, he turned to director Bob Clouse and beamed his famous cavalier smile. "We've got it!"

He wasn't alone. Warner executives, thrilled with what they had seen, had ordered the entire publicity and marketing departments thrown into high gear. Within days, word that Warner Brothers had struck the mother lode had virtually circulated the world and, as a result, movie deals again began pouring into Golden Harvest, earmarked for Bruce Lee. MGM wanted Bruce to co-star with Sophia Loren; and Warner Brothers had no less than twelve scripts ready, with hopes that Bruce could manage at least five. In addition, Bruce had been offered two movies in Hungary that purportedly would have made him the highest paid actor in the world. Most tempting of all was an incredibly imaginative deal, which the Hong Kong press stated Bruce couldn't refuse: US$100,000 per year for as long as either he or Linda should live on completion of one of five proposed scripts. This was double the amount paid annually to academy award winning actor William Holden for his landmark deal for Bridge on the River Kwai. "Frankly speaking, I am interested in this scheme," Bruce told The China Mail in a June 28 article headlined BRUCE LEE SCOOPS A SUPERSTAR SALARY. "It gives me security in the years ahead and makes taxation much easier. Besides, it doesn't bar me from working with any other studio."

Raymond Chow didn't like the sound of any of this, and there was increasing friction between the two men. In addition to many other things, it had been rumored that they had had a falling out over Bruce having negotiated a film project with Raymond's archenemy Run Run Shaw.

According to Run Run, Bruce had accepted a salary of US$400,000 to appear in a period picture centered on the life of Nin Kang Yiu, a Chinese historical hero. Whether Shaw actually had a signed contract remains a mystery, although it is true that shortly before Lee's death, Bruce appeared at the Shaw Brothers Studio for wardrobe fittings and a photography session.

Raymond wasn't the only one Bruce had begun to view with a jaundiced eye. As the final curtain began to fall,

Stirling Silliphant, Bruce Lee's long-time friend

one by one Bruce's last remaining friends were abandoned. Perhaps the most publicized had to do with Bruce's long-standing friendship with Stirling Silliphant.

According to Bob Clouse's book Bruce Lee: the Biography, while Bruce was in the U.S. for his medical tests, Silliphant had invited him to dinner, primarily to meet his fiancée, a beautiful and young Taiwanese woman named Tiana. Much to Silliphant's amazement, Bruce told him to get rid of Tiana, whom he labeled a gold digger. The phone calls went back and forth for hours, and Bruce finally told Silliphant's secretary to tell Stirling that he would not be coming to dinner because he didn't want to embarrass Linda by having her in the same company with a woman like Tiana.

The last time Stirling saw Bruce in Hong Kong, the two men had met for lunch. Bruce had brought with him two of the most gorgeous Asian women Stirling had ever seen. Following lunch, the women were to show the two men a good time at a private apartment. Besides being a happily married man, Stirling had previous plans to do a television interview, and so he declined Bruce's invitation. According to Stirling, Bruce ended up with both women, and the following day when he ran into Stirling, Bruce boasted that he had had quite a memorable afternoon with the two Oriental beauties. Stirling was not impressed and, considering how Bruce treated Tiana, for years cited the incident as an example of Bruce Lee's "curious morality." What is interesting is that right up to the day of his death Bruce had kept a personal, private file on Tiana that included several beautiful photographs of the woman.

It was also around this time that Silliphant had finally convinced Twentieth Century Fox to produce The Silent

Flute. But Bruce sneered at the entire matter and smugly told Silliphant that the studio couldn't afford him, and that above everything else he had no interest in carrying Jim Coburn on his shoulders. Ironically, this repeated almost word-for-word what Steve McQueen had said to Bruce nearly three years earlier. It wouldn't matter. The final curtain had already begun to fall.

From the day of his near-fatal collapse on May 10 to the day he died nearly ten weeks later, Bruce underwent an inexplicable and startling weight loss. Tragically, neither Bruce nor the medical professionals who examined him in May 1973 were able to pinpoint the exact cause of his excessive weight loss. Aside from the inability of the physicians to determine the cause, what troubled Bruce more was the fact that his highly defined musculature was rapidly disappearing. Metaphorically, this dramatic loss of muscle was tantamount to Superman having unknowing eaten a plate of kryptonite.

With his identity now wrapped up in his macho bad-ass image of the swashbuckling hero to the masses of downtrodden Chinese, Bruce became utterly despondent. Without his unique physical prowess, he knew his film career would be over. Never had he been known as an actor. In fact, except for Enter the Dragon, his voice was dubbed in all of his films. And although he had hoped to distinguish himself as a director in The Way of the Dragon, from a creative aspect the film had been viewed as a dismal failure.

Lee's insomnia returned. What had gone wrong? With his Chief Aim in Life literally at his fingertips, suddenly it seemed like everything was on the verge of slipping away. In a frantic attempt to keep his world from blowing apart and seeing no other way out, he turned to the one thing he believe would restore his Herculean physique—he began taking large doses of anabolic steroids.

It wasn't long before, once again, all hell broke loose at Golden Harvest Studios. Days earlier Lo Wei had referred to himself as the first million-dollar director. Although this was entirely true, Bruce didn't like the implication that Lo was taking credit for the box-office successes of The Big Boss and Fist of Fury. Having learned of Lo's presence on the studio lot, Bruce went on the hunt and discovered Lo in a private screening room where he was viewing a film with his wife and a business associate.

Suddenly the door came crashing open and Bruce stormed over to Lo Wei. Hushed silence fell over the room, then Bruce yelled at the terrified old man, "Yi kuan chin sho!" which means "beast in human clothes!" With his arms akimbo, Bruce towered over Lo Wei for what seemed an eternity, when suddenly a group of people arrived and unceremoniously dragged Bruce from the room. With synthetic male sex hormone now soaring in his bloodstream, Bruce's roid raging had returned.

Moments later, Lo's wife walked out of the screening room and confronted Bruce in Raymond's office, admonishing him for his childish and bullying behavior. Soon there was more screaming and yelling and another gathering crowd. Disgusted, Lo's wife returned to the screening room.

Ten minutes later Bruce again barged through the door and again angrily confronted the old man. This time Bruce displayed a knife, which he held only inches from Lo Wei's chest. "Do you believe I can kill you with one stab?" Bruce threatened menacingly. Lo Wei was too frightened to speak. At that moment Raymond Chow and a crowd of oth

Betty Ting-pei's apartment

ers arrived to again drag Bruce from the room.

It would not end here. Fearing for his life, Lo Wei called the police, who arrived in short order. There was more screaming and yelling, and amid the confusion, Bruce slipped the knife to Linda who smuggled it from the room. When the dust finally settled, the police agreed not to arrest Bruce if he would promise in writing that he would not physically harm or further threaten Lo Wei. Reluctantly Bruce signed such a written request.

By nightfall things got even worse. That evening Bruce, still fuming, appeared on a late night television talk show called Enjoy Yourself Tonight. Bent on showing how he could have easily defeated Lo Wei without the use of a knife, Bruce demonstrated a kung fu move on the TV interviewer. The audience was appalled, for it appeared that

Bruce had all but knocked the defenseless man halfway to kingdom come. The next morning the press raked Bruce over the coals for what it contended was yet another unnecessary act of unprovoked violence.

In an effort to quell his episodes of rage, besides his use of marijuana, Bruce began drinking heavily. Charles Lowe, who was employed as a cameraman on Enter the Dragon and frequently dined with Bruce at a local restaurant, recalled how Bruce would drink ten to twenty ceramic bottles of sake in an evening. "Near the end," Lowe added, "Bruce was often very tired and dizzy, and he looked gravely ill."

Following his frequent drinking episodes, Bruce would often find his way to the apartment of Betty Ting. On other occasions Betty would phone Bruce's house in the predawn hours, complaining that she was upset and couldn't sleep and pleading for him to come over. It was around this time that Bruce is said to have attempted to end the affair with Betty, but resumed it after she broke down and was admitted to a hospital.

Understandably the Lee marriage was in serious trouble. Besides Linda having become disenchanted with living the repressed life of the typical Oriental consort, many Chinese did not take favorably to her as Bruce's wife because she was Occidental. Of greater importance, however, was that, coupled with Bruce's unpredictable emotional outbursts, his scandalous lifestyle began to take a heavy toll on the Lee household. Every morning Linda dreaded reading the newspaper for fear of being confronted with the latest headlines of her husband's romantic liaisons, his acts of violence, and other scurrilous escapades, all of which the Lee children were also being subjected to.

But the all-encompassing issue in mid-July 1973 was that Bruce Lee, his star now cresting toward its zenith, was returning to the west, and his departing, in-your-face message was 'Don't call me, I'll call you.'

Did this mean that he had ordered Raymond to close up shop? Days earlier Bruce had publicly stated he was through making martial arts films. And what was Betty Ting, the bereaved mistress, to do? If a divorce were imminent, what would become of the children? Without Bruce, Brandon and Shannon were all Linda had. And then there was Wu Ngan, Bruce's trusted childhood friend and servant. What would become of him? Would he continue as the perpetual houseguest, or was he to be left behind in Hong Kong to once again fend for himself? And what about the triads? Were they owed money? Would there be some sort of severance payment? Perhaps they might be disposed to making an example of Bruce? And what about all the other enemies Bruce was rumored to have made? Would any of them be inclined to settle up before Bruce packed his suitcase and bid sayonara to the east? Far too many grave questions with too few answers.

While awaiting his one-way flight back to the states, Bruce grew increasingly anxious. At St. Francis Xavier College, where he had appeared to present student awards, he had introduced his international gopher Bobby Baker as his bodyguard. During the assembly a door slammed, and Bruce, utterly panic-stricken, scrambled beneath the stage. Later he showed his former teacher, Brother Gregory, the contents of a paper bag, which contained an ivory-plated Derringer loaded with two hollow-point .22 caliber bullets. In addition, Bruce often kept within arm's reach a loaded .44-Magnum, this in light of the fact that possession of a firearm in Hong Kong was an extremely serious crime.

Bruce had talked about death more than once during July 1973, and had told Linda that he would not live as long as she. When she asked him why he thought that, Bruce replied, "I don't really know. The fact is, I don't know how long I can keep this up."

As if by providence, on July 18 a typhoon struck Hong Kong, blowing down a tree in Lee's backyard, itself a bad omen, and carrying away the mirrored reflector Bruce had earlier installed on his roof to ward off bad fortune. Within forty-eight hours Bruce Lee was dead.

Officially Bruce Lee died around eleven o'clock on the evening of July 20, 1973. Although there are accountings from three different sources about what occurred that day, the basic story is simple to understand. The following is a conglomeration of these three different accountings.

Around one o'clock in the afternoon, Linda kissed Bruce goodbye at their Cumberland Road house and left to lunch with her girlfriend Rebu Hui. According to Linda, Bruce had remarked that he had plans to meet Raymond Chow later that afternoon to discuss script revisions on their next film project called Game of Death, that they would probably dine later with George Lazenby (the Australian actor who took over the James Bond role after Sean Connery), and that he would not be coming home for dinner. Linda further said that Raymond hoped Lazenby would co-star in the film.

Somewhere around two o'clock that afternoon, Raymond arrived at the Lee house, where he and Bruce worked together on the script until around four p.m. After that, they drove to the apartment of Betty Ting-pei, who was also to have a leading role in the film. At Betty's flat,

Raymond, Bruce, and Betty went over the script together, working out more details.

Having ended her luncheon with her girlfriend, Linda returned home around four o'clock, which meant she would have just missed her husband's departure with Raymond, and spent the evening exercising and watching television in Bruce's study with their two children. Aside from kissing Bruce goodbye three hours earlier and standing at his side at Queen Elizabeth Hospital some ten hours later, Linda declared she knew little about the events that happened that day at Cumberland Road and Betty Ting's apartment less than a mile away.

Around 7:30 p.m., while still at Betty's apartment, Bruce complained of a headache. Betty gave him a single tablet of Equagesic, which she later maintained was a commonly used headache remedy, and Bruce went into her bedroom to lie down. Apart from the Equagesic, Bruce took nothing by mouth except a couple of soft drinks. Ten minutes later, Raymond

The emergency area at Queen Elizabeth Hospital

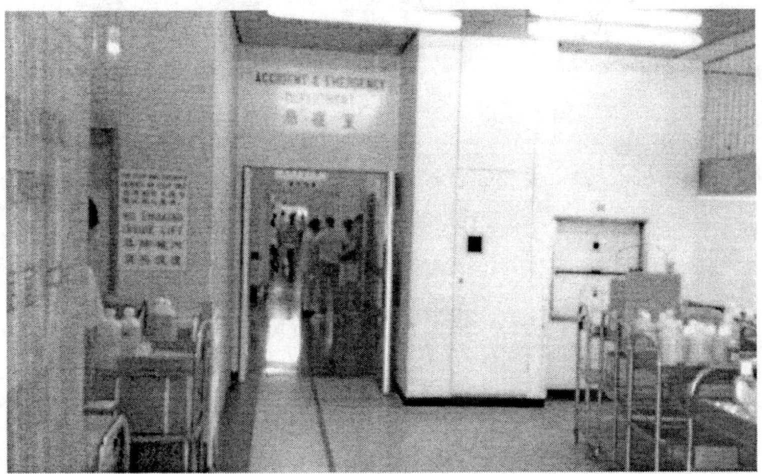

departed to meet George Lazenby for dinner at the Miramar Hotel. Bruce and Betty were to join them subsequently.

Around nine p.m. Raymond telephoned Betty's apartment from the Miramar, wanting to know why she and Bruce had not kept their dinner date with him and Lazenby. Betty and Raymond talked on the phone, and Betty informed him that she couldn't awaken Bruce.

Concerned, Raymond returned to Betty Ting's apartment and arrived around 9:30 p.m. Although Bruce appeared to be sleeping peacefully, Raymond couldn't awaken him either. Worried, he called Betty's personal physician, Dr. Chu Pho-hwye, whose line was busy. After repeated attempts, Chow finally got through to the doctor, who came immediately. Upon his arrival, Dr. Chu also attempted to awaken Bruce, but failed. With everyone now gravely concerned, someone called for an ambulance, and Bruce was rushed to Queen Elizabeth Hospital.

At around ten o'clock Raymond called Linda and requested her to go to Queen Elizabeth Hospital emergency, where fifteen minutes later Bruce arrived in an ambulance. Following a frantic attempt by a team of doctors to revive Bruce, Raymond Chow finally stepped through the hospital's main doors around 11:30 to announce to the phalanx of reporters that Bruce Lee was dead.

For the past twenty-nine years this has been the basic story of what occurred on the day Bruce Lee died in Hong Kong. It is nothing short of a miracle that it has held up this long.

Part Two

The Estate of Bruce Lee

Chapter 8

The Aftermath

"Strategy #21: The gold cicada molts its shell: This means leaving behind false appearances created for strategic purposes. Like the cicada shell, the facade remains intact, but the action is now elsewhere."

• The Japanese Art of War by Thomas Cleary

The following morning as the sun rose in the East, the news of the death of Bruce Lee, already hot on the AP wire, brought the people of Hong Kong and its neighboring communities to their knees. What had struck down the invincible King of Kung Fu? Although doctors had unofficially attributed Lee's death to brain edema, they were unable to determine what exactly had caused Lee's brain to swell.

The previous night Raymond Chow had made a totally bizarre statement to reporters, claiming that Bruce had collapsed while walking with his wife in the garden of his Kowloon Tong home. The following day the front page of the South China Morning Post had yet another offering from Raymond Chow. "BRUCE LEE WAS A SICK MAN!" the bold headlines announced. Besides remarking that Bruce had received several severe blows to the head while filming, the article stated: "Top Chinese actor Bruce Lee had been seriously ill for two months before his death, it was learned yesterday." Chow further disclosed Bruce's near-fatal collapse on May 10 at Golden Harvest Studios and related that Lee's illness was kept a closely guarded secret by his family and friends.

Why had Raymond Chow suddenly become a wealth of misinformation? Bruce's collapse on May 10 had been anything but a closely guarded secret. In addition to the Warner Brothers executives, scores of employees at Golden Harvest knew about it. The medical staffs at Baptist and St. Theresa hospitals knew about it, as did also Bruce's many friends in the United States, as well as Beverly Hills physician Dr. Harold Karpman and a large contingent of medical practitioners at UCLA Medical Center.

Nor was Bruce Lee gravely ill. Based on the extensive battery of medical tests conducted on May 25, 1973, Dr. Karpman found Bruce to be in sound physical health, and Dr. Reisbord concluded that, other than a manageable seizure disorder, there really wasn't anything wrong with Lee. And so these statements Raymond Chow made to the press on the day following Bruce's death are indeed very peculiar.

Apparently there were other skeptics. Days later, film critic Mel Tobias checked the public ambulance records at the hospital and discovered that Bruce had been taken

Crowds mourning at Bruce Lee's funeral

from 67 Beacon Hill Road, Kowloon Tong, the home of Betty Ting-pei. Within hours reporters located Raymond Chow and Linda Lee, who both persisted in evading the issue, each implying that the other was confused. Meanwhile, the angry press went looking for the sultry young Taiwanese starlet now left to fend for herself.

Betty was visibly distraught, but she swore she was telling the truth. "On Friday night when Bruce died, I was not at home. I had gone out with my mother. I last met him several months ago when we came across each other in the street." To make matters worse, several of Bruce's col leagues, along with his brother Peter, supported Betty's preposterous story. Besides the absurd notion that the ambulance attendants, who were government employees had reason to lie, Betty's neighbor had told reporters that Bruce had been a regular visitor to Betty's apartment for months. This, coupled with the hospital's inability to come up with a cause of death, cast Lee's death in a shadowy, sinister light, and the press went on a frenzy.

On Wednesday, July 25 the body of Bruce Lee, his gray face swollen and distorted like that of the deceased Elvis Presley, lay in the open bronze coffin at the Kowloon Funeral Home. Outside, over 10,000 spectators standing behind steel barriers were held back by a force of 300 police. Farther beyond, thousands more clambered precariously over the city's neon signs or perched on rooftops in what the South China Morning Post later described as a carnival.

Upon spotting the arrival of a celebrity, the spectators clapped and cheered as, one after another, the stars of the Mandarin film industry appeared: Nancy Kwan, who as Suzy Wong had once focused international attention on her homeland; Nora Miao, Bruce's leading lady, already embroiled in a whirlpool of rumors; Madame To Sam-ku, a graying actress from Bruce's child film career; George Lazenby; pop singer Sam Hui; and even director Lo Wei.

Inside the colorful parlor, a large crowd of mourners and photographers jostled together before a portrait of the dead man set on an altar surrounded by candles and incense. Amid the over 500 floral tributes from all over the world lay a wreath labeled "To Bruce from Ting-pei." Just a foot away, in front of Bruce's black-draped portrait, lay a second wreath, on which read in Chinese characters: "To my dear husband Bruce. May our marriage continue in the next world, from your grievous wife, Linda."

They were all present, that is with two glaring exceptions: Run Run Shaw from the Shaw Brothers film empire, who in a subsequent interview implied Bruce Lee had taken his own life, and the woman whose name was on everyone's lips. Heavily sedated and in bed, Betty Ting had elected to remain at her apartment. "I thought the only person who had the right to be in deep mourning in front of Bruce's coffin was his widow, Linda," Betty said tearfully. "I have high respect for her. She has many greatnesses." To the end, Bruce Lee had been a perceptive man. Betty Ting was indeed a clever woman.

When Bruce's coffin was carried from the funeral parlor, there was utter pandemonium as the police were forced to link arms and form a human chain to retrain the surging crowds. Soon reinforcements were summoned as women and children were repeatedly yanked clear of the barriers to prevent their being crushed. Old men sobbed, women of all ages fainted, and many were given medical attention for a multitude of physical ailments. Long after the funeral procession had gone, police with loudspeakers were patrolling the streets, urging people to please clear the area.

Raymond Chow wasted no time capitalizing on Bruce's death, and within ten days released The Legend of Bruce Lee throughout the Far East. The bio-documentary featured coverage of Bruce's Hong Kong funeral and tastelessly portrayed his well-publicized indiscretions, even going so far as to give a special note of thanks to Betty Ting. Writing to attorney Adrian Marshall, Linda Lee was hysterical. "Somehow this film must be stopped for obvious reasons!"

Bruce Lee's grave at Seattle's Lake View Cemetery

Betty Ting had her own exploitative ideas. Having presented herself at the doorstep of Run Run Shaw, she soon starred in a soft porn film titled Bruce Lee: His Last Days, His Last Nights (a.k.a. I Love You, Bruce Lee). The film, released in 1975 and written by Betty herself, was laughably bad and tastelessly depicted her love affair with Bruce.

Within days of Bruce's funeral, and amid a sea of speculation surrounding his death, a visibly frightened Linda Lee issued what clearly was a premature press statement: "Although we do not have a final autopsy report, I hold no suspicion of anything other than natural death. I myself do not hold any person or people responsible for his death. Fate has ways we cannot change. The only thing of importance is that Bruce is gone and will not return."

Although the fiery press had targeted numerous suspects, Betty Ting, now branded a scarlet woman, was blatantly implicated in Bruce's death. In Kuala Lumpur, angry students, convinced that their fallen idol had died of overexertion in Betty's bedroom, carried placards and truck banners reading "BETTY KILLED BRUCE!" Their hysteria was the result of the centuries-old Chinese belief that a man's life energy is contained within his sperm, and that too much sex can ultimately lead to death.

Besieged by a relentless press and a demanding public, Linda finally had no choice but to comment on Miss Ting. "So much of what is said you must not believe because it's rumor and it's absolutely untrue. Bruce was always good to me. I could not have a complaint in the world. I could not wish for a better husband." Although she had known for some time of the affair between her husband and Betty, Linda publicly credited the entire foolishness to star-tracking, further stating that as Bruce's wife, she would have known, and that she never sensed anything going on. "Besides," Linda reminisced to reporters, "Betty frequently came to our home for dinner, and the three of us would sit and enjoy Chinese food." Having heard enough, the press redoubled its efforts.

A week earlier Bruce was buried at Seattle's Lake View Cemetery. During the flight from Hong Kong, Bruce's coffin mysteriously opened and the blue dye from his suit bled onto the coffin's white silk interior. The Chinese people saw it as a grave omen. "The man will not live in peace," they proclaimed. "There are unsettled matters." The cere mony at Lake View Cemetery was a simple one. Some 300 friends, family, and spectators attended, including Steve McQueen and James Coburn. Sadly, Stirling Silliphant, the man who had unselfishly and tirelessly done more for Bruce than any single human being, purposely did not attend.

Appearing considerably less shaken now that she had returned with Bruce's body to the United States, Linda Lee told the gathering that she had "tried to share in her husband's basic beliefs, which he not only spoke but practiced in his daily life." And Warner Brothers chief Ted Ashley said, "I have a sense of sadness mingled with the realization that, while he may not have gotten up the ladder, he at least got his foot on it."

As James Coburn delivered the final eulogy, 7,000 miles away in Hong Kong the initial lab tests from the autopsy were released, and the big sensation was that marijuana had been found in Bruce's body, thereby giving birth to the latest scandal that Lee had died of a drug overdoes. Within the hour a Golden Harvest representative appealed to a crush of reporters. "Now that a great star is dead, it's the wish of most film people to let him die like a hero. The reports, if true, will undoubtedly ruin his image."

The desperate pleading from Golden Harvest was unnecessary. Two weeks later Enter the Dragon was released internationally. Despite Bruce's tarnished hero image, his onscreen performance held. At the world-renowned Grauman's Chinese Theater in Hollywood the film broke all existing box-office records in its first week, and then proceeded to sweep across the nation in a whirlwind of rave reviews. Indeed, only The Exorcist outshined it in 1973. Sadly, Bruce Lee was not alive to see one of his greatest obsessions become a reality—Enter the Dragon soundly outgrossed Steve McQueen's Getaway.

The box-office success of Enter the Dragon added fuel to the mounting public outrage at Betty Ting, and she finally threatened to sue the press if they continued publishing the rumors. "It seems that people want me to die," she told The Star. "And if this continues, I just don't want to live on. Bruce is dead. Why don't you leave it at that?"

The press was anything but touched. The following day one of the biggest newspapers in Hong Kong published a fresh list of seedy allegations, along with a front page headline challenging: "BETTY TING SUE US!" The same day the harassed woman fled into hiding.

Despite the unending denials, family and studio pleas, and threats of litigation, the suspicious death of Bruce Lee remained in the headlines. Upon inquiring into Bruce's finances, The Star soon disclosed yet another allegation: when Lee died, he was virtually broke. According to The Star, most of his Concord stock holdings, in addition to his Kowloon Tong home, were in the name of his butler, Wu Ngan. Moreover, it was claimed that Bruce's much heralded Rolls Royce had never been ordered. With Linda having again gone into seclusion, the press finally cornered Raymond Chow, who scoffed at the stories. "Bruce had enough money when he died," Chow announced to the world. "He could well afford a Rolls Royce and a house among other things."

In late August, police were called to investigate a suspicious brown paper bag believed to contain a bomb and upon which had been written: "Betty Ting knows the cause of Bruce Lee's death!" Bomb scares involving similar pack ages continued. Finally, with no end in sight to the slander and allegations destroying more than a hapless Taiwanese actress, the British government had no choice but to order an official inquiry into the death of Bruce Lee.

CHAPTER 9

The Coroner's Inquest

"The great masses of people will more easily fall victim to a big lie than to a small one."

• Adolf Hitler

The summer of 1973 was perhaps the worst time in history to turn up mysteriously dead in Hong Kong, especially if one had a long list of influential enemies. In the early 1970s, when corruption was at its peak in the Hong Kong government, it was estimated that 35 percent of all Chinese policemen were triad members. It was around this time that British police commander Peter Godber fled to England to avoid an investigation into how he accumulated $880,000 in a Swiss bank account when his policeman's salary had paid him only $180,000 over twenty years.

Embarrassed by the unearthing of Commander Godber as Hong Kong's chief law enforcement officer, the

British, on direct orders from London, formally began to investigate police corruption. Soon it was discovered that five key Chinese staff sergeants inside the Triad Bureau, which was then the police department directly responsible for investigating and prosecuting triad crimes, were themselves triad members. The ringleader of the group was Sergeant Lui Lok, a highly decorated officer with an excellent arrest history. Junior policemen referred to him as "Tai Lo," the Chinese equivalent of the Mafia's godfather. Lui Lok and his four underworld associates were on triad payrolls, receiving a percentage of the gambling, vice and drug operations to which they turned a blind eye. The rampant payoffs amounted to hundreds of millions of dollars. Lui Lok is called "the 600-million-dollar man," the estimated size of his illegal fortune. He is one of forty ex-Hong Kong police millionaires living today in Taiwan.

On September 17, 1973 the formal inquest into the death of Bruce Lee opened at Tsunwan, with witness testimony begin given over the next four days. Throngs of Chinese eager to hear Betty Ting's testimony packed the spectator gallery and overflowed down the courthouse steps. In an effort to suppress the anxious crowds, police erected steel barriers, while inside Coroner Egbert Tung was busy compiling what he prayed would be a complete and accurate accounting of Bruce Lee's final hours. Until now, the colony's longest running sideshow had been an inquiry into the alleged suicide of Inspector John MacLennan who, according to official police reports, shot himself in the chest five times.

Generally speaking, the three central figures who were around Bruce Lee on the day of his death—Linda Lee,

Betty Ting, and Raymond Chow—held to the basic story, although there were several glaring inconsistencies.

As to when people came and went from either Cumberland Road or Betty Ting's apartment a mile away on Beacon Hill, no one could agree. Disturbing to many, the sworn testimony of the three principal witnesses seemed to arbitrarily toss out an hour here and an hour there.

To begin with, Linda testified that she left the Lee home at one o'clock and returned three hours later at four. Although she was vehement about Raymond Chow arriving at the house at two p.m. (although presumably she wasn't there), Chow swore that he arrived no earlier than three. As to Bruce and Raymond driving to Betty's, Chow declared that they arrived at Beacon Hill at five, to which Betty agreed. Nevertheless, Linda was adamant that Chow arrived at Betty's a full hour earlier at four. In any event, there appeared to be a "floating hour," which clearly was very important to these witnesses. Curiously this was at a time when the coroner had not yet officially committed to an exact time of death.

When Betty Ting testified, she denied under oath that she and Bruce had any previous plans to have dinner with Raymond Chow and George Lazenby, but that at around seven p.m. she, Bruce, and Raymond decided to have dinner at a Japanese restaurant. Linda had earlier said that Bruce told her on the day of his death that he was having dinner that evening with Chow and Lazenby, the primary purpose being to coax Lazenby into doing Game of Death. Two years later, however, Linda told reporters in Hong Kong that on that fateful day, Chow, Lazenby, and

Bruce had met at Betty's.

What is bothersome about this entire matter of the all-encompassing "dinner with Lazenby" is that Raymond Chow had stated to the press on July 21 that he and Lazenby had days earlier signed a contract regarding Game of Death. If this was true, then this business about Bruce and Betty coming to the Miramar in hopes of convincing Lazenby to make the picture is clearly a ruse.

Unquestionably the most troublesome issue was the matter of the phone call that allegedly occurred between Betty and Raymond. Betty stated that she called Raymond at the Miramar Hotel at 8:20 p.m., which was a mere twenty minutes after she alleges Raymond left her apartment. Chow's dinner with Lazenby wasn't scheduled for another and ten minutes, yet she was already calling Chow at the Miramar dining room to tell him that Bruce was still sleeping. According to Betty, Chow told her to let him sleep. Forty-five minutes later she called the Miramar again and told Chow the same thing. Again, Chow told her to let Bruce sleep and that he would drive to her apartment following his dinner with Lazenby. The problem with this scenario is that if Bruce were merely sleeping, why would Chow be going back to Betty's? And why at that late hour?

Not surprisingly, Chow had a completely different version. He claimed he never received a call from Betty at all. According to Raymond, he called Betty at 9:30 p.m., wanting to know why she and Bruce had not kept their dinner engagement.

Then there is Linda's recollection. Although she wasn't at Betty's or the Miramar Hotel, for the past twenty-nine years she has steadfastly supported Raymond

Chow's version of events.

In retrospect, what seems likely is that Bruce was planning to dine out alone with Betty, after which they were tentatively planning to join Raymond and Lazenby at the Miramar for dessert or an after-dinner drink. For whatever reason, Bruce and Betty never left Betty's apartment, and when Betty became aware of Bruce's ill condition around 9:30, she telephoned Raymond at the Miramar, simply because she knew he was there.

As the courtroom drama twisted like a slalom course, cresting in its third day, the sweltering heat and suffocating humidity began to wear on everyone's patience, and tempers began to flare. Fed up with the soap opera of conflicting testimony, the crowds grew restless, and when Raymond was questioned about the bizarre story he had handed the press the night of Bruce's death, things really got tentative. In one sweeping and bold gesture, Chow flatly denied telling reporters on July 20 that Bruce had died at home. Outraged, the crowd rose to their feet, and there were boos from the packed press benches.

The next bombshell to rock Tsunwan came when Linda Lee took the stand and confirmed the widely circulating rumor that her husband had used marijuana. The subsequent speculation that Bruce had died of a drug overdoes, however, was short-lived, owing to the testimony of two key witnesses.

The first was that of government chemist Dr. Lam King-leung, who testified that only a small amount of marijuana had been found in Lee's stomach and small intestine. The second, and more critical testimony, was that of Professor Ronald Teare of London University's Forensic

Medicine Department, who had flown to Hong Kong specifically to give his expert opinion that he considered the marijuana found in Lee's body "about as significant as if I had been told Lee had taken a cup of tea or coffee."

Professor Teare was quite a remarkable witness. According to his testimony, he had been a specialist of forensic medicine for thirty-five years, during which time he had performed over 90,000 autopsies and given evidence at 18,000 inquests. This was one busy man. Figuring a five-day work week, with not one single day's absence for either vacation or illness, Teare was able to average ten autopsies per day, in addition to slipping in appearances at two separate inquest hearings every working day for thirty-five years! And this was in London where the police don't even carry guns! In any event, coupled with Dr. Lam's comments, Professor Teare's testimony was enough to defuse the theory that Bruce had died of a drug overdose.

There are several elements of Teare's testimony that are worthy of comment. The first is that he ridiculed the theory that marijuana caused Bruce's collapse on May 10, as well as Lee's state of unconsciousness and subsequent death on July 20. As a rebuttal, in his sworn deposition Dr. Harold Karpman testified that the marijuana (1-milligram) Bruce had ingested on May 10 could very well have caused Bruce's convulsions and subsequent, near-fatal brain edema. Secondly, although odds are that Professor Teare is probably correct in his view that marijuana in the amount found in Bruce's system on July 20 could not have caused his death, it is important to note that Teare is talking about untainted marijuana that has not been laced. Lastly,

Teare's testimony that it was his professional opinion that the two events of May 10 and July 20 were purely coincidental was completely unsubstantiated.

As the inquest drew to a close, the crowds diminished. It seemed they had initially come to see Betty Ting, Linda Lee, and Raymond Chow, but, following the court's dismissal of the three key witnesses, quickly became bored with the complex scientific analysis of the wide assortment of prescription drugs Bruce had been taking. As a result, by the final days only a few reporters bothered showing up at all, and the barricades were removed.

After three weeks of investigation, the court claimed to have before it the true and complete story according to Lee's friends, colleagues and relatives, and pages of medical opinion. On September 23, Mr. Egbert Tung delivered a verdict of "death by misadventure," which technically is a shade away from "accidental death," further clarifying that Bruce Lee had died from acute cerebral edema as a result of a hypersensitivity to either meprobamate or aspirin, or a combination of the two, found in a single tablet of Equagesic given to him by Betty Ting.

Presumably the court and police authorities were satisfied. Clearly the people of Hong Kong, and many in the United States and elsewhere, were not. Amid the eerie diorama were too many cover-ups, too many half-truths and whitewashed relationships, too many shadows and rattling skeletons.

It is nothing less than unearthly that the setting of the Kowloon funeral parlor was practically identical to the one depicted in the opening scenes of Fist of Fury in which

Chapter Nine

Bruce, dressed in the same blue suit that he wore to his Seattle grave, falls grief-stricken on the coffin of his dead kung fu master.

"Would you tell me what teacher died of?" Lee asked bitterly in the opening scene.

"It was pneumonia. That is what the autopsy said," his fellow student replied.

"And you believe that?"

CHAPTER 10

The Autopsy

The morning after Lee's death, police homicide detectives in Hong Kong began checking into Bruce's drug connections and later sent to the laboratory four tablets, three glasses, and two soft drink bottles they had obtained from Betty Ting's apartment. Their investigation, however, would be severely hampered, due primarily to the fact that Linda had since removed Bruce's body from Hong Kong jurisdiction when she transported Bruce's body to Seattle for burial. Had the Hong Kong police later obtained evidence pointing to foul play, in all likelihood it subsequently would have been necessary to exhume Bruce's body in the U.S. to conduct further forensic test. Without Linda Lee's permission, this would have been practically impossible.

Coroner Tung's verdict that Bruce Lee had died as a result of hypersensitivity to a single table of Equagesic was as wildly speculative as the Warren Commission Report. In sharp contrast, however, to the Kennedy assassination, Tung's verdict further put an end to any criminal investigation into Bruce Lee's death. This is not to suggest that

Coroner Tung or anyone else purposely quashed an investigation. But the truth was, in the summer of 1973 Hong Kong was painfully analogous to Los Angeles in the days surrounding the O.J. Simpson and Rodney King verdicts, and the authorities simply wanted the whole ugly matter to go away. To that end, Dr. R.R. Lycette's autopsy was helpful in that its findings were uneventful.

Initially, Dr. Lycette examined the physical body itself. The back of Lee's throat was clear and normal, and the vocal cords were free of swelling. The covering of the lungs showed a degree of minor hemorrhaging and moderate congestion. Additionally, there was some fluid in the lungs, and microscopic tests showed internal congestion of the vessels, although there was no evidence of pneumonia. In some areas blood had burst through the vessels and entered the air space of the lungs. All other organs, including the heart, were normal. Summarily, any of the above findings could have belonged to a man with a common cold.

Dr. Lycette then sent samples of the stomach contents, urine, blood, liver, kidney, small intestine, and the colon to a laboratory in Hong Kong, where they were examined by Dr. Lam. In addition, samples were sent to laboratories in Australia and New Zealand. Dr. Lam noted that .5 milligrams of marijuana were found in Lee's stomach and .4 milligrams in the small intestine. Tests were also done for trace metals, specifically mercury and lead, as well as alcohol, morphine, and a few other organic chemicals, but the results were negative.

Dr. Lam also searched for illicit drugs in Lee's body, particularly Spanish Fly, but, besides marijuana, found none. Moreover, Lam found no evidence of the drug

Dilantin, which had been prescribed to Lee eight weeks earlier to control seizures. Although Lam did not elaborate on which drugs he had tested for, it seems fair to assume that his list would have included cocaine.

As Dr. Lycette placed his signature on Lee's autopsy, nothing seemed out of the ordinary, except one thing. Although Lycette had noted an absence of any skull injuries, Lee's brain was swollen like a sponge and weighed 1,575 grams compared with the normal 1,400 grams. Because the blood vessels of the brain were intact and were unblocked, Lycette concluded that Lee had not died of cerebral stroke or brain hemorrhage. As to the fatal brain edema, this could have occurred in a matter of minutes or over an entire day. In Lee's case, it was Dr. Lycette's opinion that it developed very rapidly.

The conclusion that Bruce Lee died from cerebral edema has never been challenged by anyone. The problem has been in accepting that a single tablet of Equagesic is what caused the fatal edema.

Over the past twenty-nine years, many have raised the question of whether there was a direct relationship between Lee's collapse on May 10 and his death ten weeks later on July 20. If one were conducting a criminal investigation into Lee's death and could positively link these two incidents together, it most assuredly would have opened the door to the theory that someone had attempted to kill Bruce Lee on May 10 and, having failed, made another attempt ten weeks later that succeeded.

What do we know about the May 10 incident? We've been told that Bruce, while in the dubbing room at Golden Harvest, felt nauseated. Excusing himself, he then grew weak, and perhaps fainted, in a nearby restroom. Twenty minutes later he regained his strength and returned to the dubbing room, where he collapsed. Within minutes he vomited and began convulsing. Another twenty minutes elapsed, after which he was taken to Baptist Hospital where he was found to have a very high fever and was having difficulty breathing. Soon the doctors detected brain swelling, which they were able to control by administering the drug Mannitol. An hour and a half later, Bruce was revived and, following a period of amnesia, returned to normal.

Is this scenario in any way similar to what occurred on the evening of July 20? Did Bruce feel nauseated? According to Raymond Chow and Betty Ting, Bruce only complained of a headache. Did he faint? Again according to Raymond and Betty, Bruce went into Betty's bedroom to lie down. Immediately after that Raymond left, and the implication derived from Betty's testimony is that Bruce fell asleep. Did he throw up? Doubtful. Dr. Lycette found marijuana in Bruce's stomach. What about difficulty breathing? Only Betty would know, and she never mentioned it. What about fever? Bruce was dead on arrival at Queen Elizabeth Hospital and would have had a subnormal temperature. Sketchy. Fragmented. But the brain swelling was present on both days, as was also the ingestion of marijuana.

Let's examine more closely the coroner's verdict that Bruce's death was caused by his hypersensitivity to a single tablet of Equagesic. According to Betty Ting, she gave Bruce a commonly used headache pill, which had been prescribed to her by her doctor for years. This, in itself, is troublesome. To begin with, Equagesic is not prescribed for headache, but is used to treat anxiety and stress in patients with muscu loskeletal diseases, rheumatic disorders, or injury to soft tissues such as muscles and ligaments. Based on Bruce's history of back and joint pain, it is understandable that he might have taken Equagesic. The notion that Betty had been taking it for years is perplexing, in that she has no medical history of musculoskeletal disorders. Secondly, Equagesic is a controlled substance that is both physically and psychologically addicting. It isn't likely that any responsible physician would have prescribed this drug to Betty for years. Moreover, according to its manufacturer, Wyeth Laboratories, withdrawal from Equagesic may cause the return of symptoms of anxiety, anorexia, insomnia, or withdrawal reactions of vomiting, ataxia, and tremors.

The symptoms almost jump out at you, don't they? Insomnia, a common complaint of Bruce's for well over a year. Anxiety, another. Anorexia, Bruce's history of weight loss and dehydration. Is it possible that Bruce was a more frequent user of Equagesic than we've previously been told, and that he was taking the drug to combat anxiety?

Although this may shed light on some of Bruce's other problems, Equagesic was not what caused Bruce's death. To prove this conclusively, we need to delve further into the drug, itself, as well as Bruce Lee's medical history.

Chemically a single tablet of Equagesic contains 200 milligrams of meprobamate and 325 milligrams of aspirin. In that Bruce was a frequent user of Darvon Compound 65, of which each tablet contains 389 milligrams of aspirin, the possibility that Bruce's death could have been the result of his ingesting 325 milligrams of aspirin is extremely remote.

Moreover, we have only to examine the testimony of Professor Ronald Teare. You remember him. He's the forensic expert who flew all the way from London to tell Coroner Tung that the presence of marijuana found in Lee's body was about as significant as if he had been told that Lee had taken a cup of tea or coffee. If that kind of testimony is strong enough to equate marijuana to a cup of tea or coffee, then it is strong enough to rule out the significance of aspirin, as well.

Which leaves 200 milligrams of meprobamate as the only possibility of a smoking gun. A single tablet more innocent than a spoonful of NyQuil. How in the world did it become so powerful? The answer lies in Dr. Lycette's red herring theory about Bruce Lee being hypersensitive to Equagesic.

Summarily, Dr. Lycette stated that although an allergy requires some prior exposure to an agent, hypersensitivity does not. He went on to say that a person can simply be hypersensitive to a substance, or hypersensitivity can be developed to a substance to which a person has been previously exposed.

Sounds confusing, doesn't it? Here's a simple, practical example of how it works, according to Dr. Lycette: the first time you came down with poison oak you were hypersensitive. The second and third time you were most likely allergic, in which case you're going to be scratching and applying Calamine lotion for a week to ten days. On the other hand, there is a remote possibility that your body has become fatally hypersensitive to the leaf. If this is true then it is entirely possible that you could have literally romped in the stuff all summer, even put it in your salad, without one single itch, and then one day you barely brushed up against a single tiny leaf and, as a result, you suddenly found your self swollen up like a weather balloon and in a horrifying fight for your life!

Now do you know anyone who has had this experience? I don't either. So how did this testimony get into the record? Why didn't Dr. Lycette and the others attribute Bruce's death to his being allergic to meprobamate rather than hypersensitive? The reason is that in order to have accepted such a theory, one would have also had to accept the premise that Bruce Lee had previously taken meprobamate without life-threatening consequences. And clearly this would have been a far more difficult theory for the coroner, not to mention the press and the public, to swallow.

Recall that ten months earlier Bruce had consulted with Dr. Otto Au on October 5, 1972. His chief complaints were (1) excessive sweating, (2) acne, (3) weight loss, and (4) sunken cheeks. Six weeks later surgery was performed to remove the sweat glands under Bruce's arms. Postoperatively Bruce was advised on the applications of acne lotion, instructed to eat a balanced diet supplemented with vitamins, and rest. Three injections of Ledecort were given to soften the scars, and two prescriptions were ordered - Penbritin and Miltown. Penbritin is a common antibiotic. What is Miltown? It's another name for meprobamate! And like Equagesic, Miltown is suggested for the management of anxiety disorders or for shot term relief of symptoms of anxiety. A single table contains 200 or 400 or 600 milligrams of meprobamate depending on the strength prescribed. Recall that a single table of Equagesic contains 200 milligrams of meprobamate, which is equal to the smallest tablet does of Miltown. As an aside, one has to question why Bruce had been prescribed Miltown, which is suggested for anxiety management, postoperatively for the removal of sweat glands.

In any case, the important point is that Bruce Lee was hardly a stranger to meprobamate. Was Dr. Lycette aware of this? No. Curiously, at the coroner's inquest only Bruce's current medications were considered. The matter of Bruce having previously taken meprobamate surfaced months later in the office of the attorneys who were challenging Bruce's life insurance.

Unquestionably, the greatest and most obvious flaw in Dr. Lycette's theory that Bruce Lee died of a hypersensitivity to a single table of Equagesic is one of sequence. The problem is that Bruce ingested the Equagesic after he com

Why was Equagesic singled out as the lone suspect?

plained of a headache, which presumably was caused by the onset of his brain starting to swell with fluid. And it was after he noted the onset of the headache that he died. This is similar to the sequence of the events of May 10. Bruce felt ill and then afterwards lapsed into a coma and began convulsing. On July 20 Bruce did not take the Equagesic and then become ill. He felt ill before he took the Equagesic.

Here is the same problem on very simple terms: Your close friend comes to you around noon complaining of an upset stomach, mild fever, and headache. Believing he is perhaps coming down with the flu, you put him to bed and give him a bowl of your grandmother's age-old chicken soup. This isn't the first time you've given this soup to your friend. You've done such a favor on numerous occasions in the past, all with success. Two hours later, you friend, who presumably had been in superb physical health, is found dead from a massive stroke. A week later, when an official autopsy is unable to come up with a cause of death, a forensic specialist flies in from Lithuania and announces to the world that your friend died of being hypersensitive to your grandmother's chicken soup. As utterly preposterous as this sounds, this is the logic used to reach the final verdict given at the close of the inquest into the death of Bruce Lee.

And finally, with all the prescription and illicit drugs Bruce was taking at the time of his death, why single out Equagesic as the lone suspect?

Dr. Harold Karpman was one of many who were not convinced. Having reviewed Bruce Lee's autopsy, the esteemed physician gave the following sworn statement regarding Dr. Lycette's theory:

Q: And I'm just curious as to what your professional opinion was regarding Lee's autopsy?
A: I was left in limbo as to what exactly it meant, and still I don't know what really was the cause of it.

Clearly Coroner Tung's verdict that Bruce Lee's death was caused by a single tablet of Equagesic is as leaky as the hull of the Queen Elizabeth that sits rusting at the bottom of the Hong Kong harbor. Consequently, to this day much of Bruce's life, particularly his final three years in Hong Kong, remains cloaked in secrecy. Perhaps some of the mystery can be uncovered by examining what went on around Bruce after his death. This is the primary objective of the next five chapters.

CHAPTER 11

War Declared

Shortly after Bruce's Seattle funeral, Linda placed her two children in the care of her sister and in September 1973 returned to Hong Kong to testify at the coroner's inquest. There were other problems that began to surface around this time that were potentially cataclysmic by comparison to those unfolding inside Coroner Tung's heated courtroom.

At the time of his death, Bruce Lee was represented by the prestigious Hong Kong law firm of Lo and Lo. Upon her husband's death, however, Linda fired Lo and Lo and rehired Adrian Marshall, whose legal services Bruce had abruptly ended in 1972 for reasons that have never been satisfactorily explained.

There were some surprises, however. Upon his hasty arrival in Hong Kong, Marshall called Lo and Lo and requested they send over Bruce's will. According to Lo and Lo, Bruce didn't have a will. Marshall demanded to know why. Lo and Lo didn't have an answer and didn't feel they owed him one, even if they had.

Questioned by reporters, Linda stated that Bruce had

died without having made a will because, in his supreme health, he felt that a will was unnecessary. They were sorry they'd asked.

Marshall was furious. Although it appeared that Bruce had led several people to believe otherwise, he had never drawn up a will, which meant that he had died intestate. Although in the United States the estate of a deceased individual who dies intestate legally passes to the spouse, according to the probate law in Hong Kong, Bruce's two minor children were to inherit Bruce's entire estate, not his widow Linda.

Following an exhaustive analysis of the legal problem, Marshall, in a bold and unprecedented maneuver, argued before a California judge that Bruce was a resident of the state of California, even though he did not own property in California and was living with his wife and children in Hong Kong at the time of his death. It worked. Petitioning the California superior court, Linda now contended that neither Bruce's son Brandon, nor his daughter Shannon, had any interest in their father's estate.

You will recall that not long after Bruce's death The Star began to pry into his finances and soon reported that when Lee died he was virtually broke. This was partly true. What they should have reported was that when Bruce died, he was owed a lot of money. That is, maybe he was owed the money, this according to his business partner Raymond Chow. The central issue revolved around the assets, if any, of Concord Productions, which was the company Bruce and Raymond had formed in 1972 to produce The Way of the Dragon and co-produce Enter the Dragon, the latter of which had not yet been released.

From a standpoint of business leverage, Chow was in an excellent position. He was rich. Famous. Influential. He was a very busy and extremely difficult man to reach. He was a Chinese facing a notoriously complaisant and naive Caucasian woman alone with two small children, ostensibly penniless, and 7,000 miles away in Seattle. Chow's biggest gun, however, was that he held all the money and the corporate books.

Raymond Chow had Linda over a barrel, and the notion of her being out in the cold had Marshall seeing red. Together Linda and Adrian went looking for bank accounts by phone and by letter, either in the name of Bruce Lee or Concord. Linda had felt that the accounts could be at Bank of America. There weren't any. Just like there wasn't a will. The years of knowing little about her husband's personal life and his business dealings were now taking their toll, and it was extremely embarrassing.

In the absence of any additional accounts, this meant that, with the exception of approximately US$3,000 in a Bank of Hong Kong checking account, US$15,000 in a savings account, and a $5,000 note from the sale of their Bel Air home, which in total wouldn't pay for Bruce's funeral expenses, Linda Lee was penniless. There was, however, the US$4,000 monthly living expense allotment the Lees had been receiving from Golden Harvest for the past two years. Surely that would pay the rent and put food on the Lee table while everyone figured out all these financial matters. Of course, one might suppose that the money could have been used for a legal retainer should Linda been inclined to employ the services of a powerful Hong Kong law firm?

It didn't matter. On the day following Bruce's death,

and without any advance warning, Raymond Chow canceled the Lees' living expense allotment and left town.

Linda Lee and Adrian Marshall had no choice but to engage Chow in all-out war, and in order to do this they needed money. At the time of Bruce's death, 41 Cumberland Road—this alleged dragon slayer with a sinister reputation of being a vicious financial equalizer—was legally owned by Bruce's corporation, Lo Yuen Enterprises, Ltd. In fact, it was the corporation's only asset. When Marshall located Bruce's corporate books, which he subsequently demanded from the offices of Golden Harvest, he wasted no time telexing Realtor Mildred Poon in Hong Kong with orders to sell 41 Cumberland Road for US$180,000, and to use the simplest, quickest, and cheapest method.

It would be nine months before the house sold, ironically at a loss. One might have predicted that the Hong Kong home of Bruce Lee would have soared in value, but such was not the case. Perhaps the house had indeed been jinxed, and few wanted any part of it.

Meanwhile, and based on the anticipated equity income of US$40,000 from the sale of the Cumberland house, Linda and Adrian hired the accounting firm of Johnson, Stokes & Masters (JSM), which became responsible for the administration of Bruce's estate. In addition, the accounting firm of Peat, Marwick, Mitchell & Co. (PMM&CO), with offices based in Hong Kong and Beverly Hills, was brought in to address the complex tax problem of estate death taxes and the prospect of Linda's future estate tax planning.

With all the heavy hitters now firmly in place, Adrian Marshall made another run at Raymond Chow.

Months later, Marshall wrote to Richard Heller at the Los Angeles office of PMM&CO and, regarding his battle with Raymond Chow, gave Heller the sorrowful news on how Marshall had either struck out at the plate or had been thrown out stealing second.

In response to Heller's request for additional information about Bruce Lee's salary arrangement for 1972, Marshall found himself up against an attorney's worst nightmare. Following negotiations in Los Angeles in 1972 with Raymond Chow, only informal oral agreements had resulted. Essentially neither Raymond Chow nor Concord had ever signed any document that would have firmly established a formal obligation to pay any moneys to Bruce Lee either as a salary or bonus. After three trips to Hong Kong, God only knows how many frustratingly exhaustive meetings with Hong Kong lawyers, accountants, business personnel and others, Adrian Marshall found himself taking a standing eight count. Considering the lack of proof of the existence of anything other than what Marshall deemed as virtually unenforceable oral agreements between Bruce Lee and Raymond Chow, Marshall concluded that there would be no additional payments forthcoming of either salary or bonuses.

For the moment, Raymond Chow was totally unwilling to pay any money to Linda and he wasn't about to be backed into a corner by any threat of litigation. This was Hong Kong, not Beverly Hills. Having been soundly defeated by Raymond Chow's dream team, Marshall returned to the United States.

Among a host of other items, the central problem was that CPA Heller was trying to explain to the IRS why

Bruce Lee should not be charged back taxes on income he never received in 1972 and 1973. According to Heller, the snag was numerous bookkeeping entries that were made by Bruce's business associate Raymond Chow. Although one could easily note where Chow had made large financial entries in his corporate books in Bruce's name, it appeared that the money had never been paid to Bruce. Had this money been used to support Bruce's mistress Betty Ting and her extravagant lifestyle? Then again, the possibility existed that these entries were triad payoffs. And if that is what they were, one surely couldn't officially, or even legitimately, claim them as tax deductions.

Things got worse. Heller approached a Mr. Meickle of the Internal Revenue Service and pleaded his case. The accounts of Concord Productions Ltd. and other Hong Kong corporations were written up after Bruce Lee's death. PMM&CO's Hong Kong office had prepared financial statements from these accounts, and it was these financial statements that led Heller to conclude that there had been an omission of income. Since the accounts were not drawn up until after Bruce Lee's death and, according to Heller's own words, Mr. Chow's probity was for other reasons not beyond questioning, the IRS must view Chow's books to be erroneous in a number of respects, but particularly in regard to Bruce Lee's salary arrangements. Surely one has to ask what exactly, according to Heller, were the "other reasons" why Raymond Chow's honesty and uprightness were "not beyond questioning."

There was more trouble. The Hong Kong Bank of California had been appointed by the probate court as administrator of the Estate of Bruce Lee. This made it extremely difficult for Adrian Marshall to speak with any authority, which prompted Linda Lee, upon the advice of Marshall, to request that she be appointed administrator in place of the Hong Kong Bank of California. Unfortunately, the court would not grant her request for another three months.

Jeffrey S. Weeks, the Trust Administration Officer of the Hong Kong Bank of California in Beverly Hills, wasn't inclined to empower Adrian Marshall prematurely, and he practically said as much in a letter to Richard Heller over at PMM&CO. As far as Weeks was concerned, the bank was going to continue acting as the administrator of the Estate of Bruce Lee. Because Marshall had never completed any negotiations with the bank, he was, according to Weeks, acting without any legal authority at all.

Within minutes, Heller telexed Marshall's law partner Bryant Burton and told him that he found the bank's position difficult to believe. Did Burton know anything about Marshall crossing swords with the bank's appointed estate representative Ben Mancini? Adrian was already back in Hong Kong with Linda. Long into the dead of night the telexes went back and forth between the Los Angeles office of Peat, Marwich, Mitchell & Co., specifically to their overseas representative Mr. J.B. Osborne, and the branch offices of the Hong kong Bank of California both in the U.S. and Hong Kong. When the dust finally settled, Marshall found himself staring at the same problem. The bank insisted that, empowered by Linda, Marshall had flexed his muscle prematurely.

"Marshall was extremely controlling of Linda Lee," Mancini recently recalled from his home in northern

California. "And it was very apparent to me that she was the type of woman that would be very susceptible to that sort of man. But the real problem was that Marshall refused to cooperate with the bank and he just wanted to control everything and I just couldn't put the bank in that position."

Hours later a perplexing, if not alarming, telex was sent to J.B. Osborne from Richard Heller, who had been attempting to resolve the dustup between Marshall and Mancini: "Attention J.B. Osborne for Adrian Marshall / stop / Mancini says he will resign for five thousand dollars in cash / stop / otherwise he will litigate / stop / best regards R. Heller."

What did Mancini have to offer Marshall that was worth $5,000 in cash, which today would be the equivalent of over $30,000? Ben Mancini was the court-appointed administrator of the estate, and Marshall was the attorney for the estate. Both had strong ethical and moral obligations to uphold, and yet here was Mancini offering Marshall this midnight under-the-table payoff via global telex. Most unusual. Yet another red flag.

CHAPTER 12

Lloyds of London and AIA

Nothing will cast suspicion on the untimely death of an individual more than questionable life insurance, and within days of Coroner Tung opening the official inquest into the death of Bruce Lee, both AIA and Lloyds of London announced that they were not going to pay.

Quite understandably, the attorneys representing Lloyds of London had several problems with the million-dollar policy they had issued just ten weeks before Lee's death, in particular the application form, whereupon it was alleged that Bruce Lee had made numerous misrepresentations in order to induce the insurance company to issue the policy.

To begin with, the attorneys challenged the fact that Lee never disclosed his prior back injury in 1970, which required him to take occasional doses of a pain medication commonly given to terminally ill cancer patients. Second, they charged that Lee had suffered numerous physical injuries while filming deadly fight sequences. Third, Lee had contemplated journeying beyond the limits of Malaya.

Chapter Twelve

Lee's Lloyds of London policy

EDWARD LUMLEY & SONS (SINGAPORE) PTE. LTD.

LONDON PRINCIPALS:
EDWARD LUMLEY & SONS LTD.
LUMLEY HOUSE,
ST. MARY AXE,
LONDON, E. C. 3.
AND AT
LLOYD'S

ASSOCIATED COMPANIES
IN
AUSTRALIA, CANADA,
FRANCE, NEW ZEALAND,
SOUTH AFRICA AND U.S.A.

(INCORPORATED IN THE REPUBLIC OF SINGAPORE)
INSURANCE BROKERS
INSURANCES EFFECTED
AT
LLOYD'S
LONDON
32A, RAFFLES PLACE,
P.O. BOX 111,
PHONE: 94823-5
SINGAPORE

TELEGRAMS: "OBVERT"
ASSOCIATED COMPANY
IN
MALAYSIA
EDWARD LUMLEY & SONS (MALAYSIA) SDN. BHD.
3RD FLOOR, STRAITS TRADING BUILDING,
LEBOH PASAR BESAR,
P. O. Box 396
PHONE: 29-9921
KUALA LUMPUR

CHARTERED BANK CHAMBERS
BEACH STREET,
P.O. BOX 373,
PHONE: 61586
PENANG.

15th May, 1973

Certificate No. ZHA.3/145/0002
ZHA.3/PA/0001

THIS CERTIFICATE OF INSURANCE IS ISSUED IN ACCORDANCE with the Contract granted to EDWARD LUMLEY & SONS (SINGAPORE) PTE. LTD. through the intermediary of EDWARD LUMLEY & SONS LTD. Lloyd's Brokers, by certain Underwriting Members of Lloyd's London (hereinafter called "the Underwriters") whose names and the proportion underwritten by each of them are specified in the signed copy of the said Contract which may be inspected at any reasonable time at the office of EDWARD LUMLEY & SONS (SINGAPORE) PTE. LTD.

WHEREAS Mr. Bruce Lee,
41, Cumberland Road, Kowloon, Hongkong

(hereinafter called "the Assured") has paid or agreed to pay premium or consideration as detailed hereunder to insure from loss or damage on the terms and condition of LLOYD'S PERSONAL ACCIDENT POLICY (K.2 SCALE IV FORM) - NMA.1089 policy form as incorporated herein from 30.4.73 to 30.4.74 (at 4 p.m. Local Standard Time) and for such further period or periods as may be mutually agreed upon, ~~with 15 days grace after expiry for renewal~~

xx £400,000.- ON (STERLING POUNDS FOUR HUNDRED THOUSAND ONLY).

On the above Assured
Occupation:- Film Maker
Age:- 32 yrs.

Subject to the terms and conditions of Lloyd's
K.2 Scale IV Form as attached.

All Premiums and Claims (if any) payable in SINGAPORE.

In relation to all claims arising under this Insurance the Underwriters submit to the jurisdiction of all the Courts of Singapore. They agree that service of legal process and of any notifications required under this Policy upon Messrs. Donaldson & Burkinshaw, 1st Floor, Mercantile Bank Building, Singapore, shall be good and sufficient service and shall be equivalent to personal service upon them and each of them. They further agree that they will all abide and be bound by the ultimate decision in any action brought against any of them in relation to such matters as aforesaid.

This Certificate is issued subject to the terms of the policy, conditions of which are shown overleaf. The amount of premium mentioned hereto is the amount due to the Underwriters, whose names will be supplied on application, and any discounts and/or commission allowed by them are to be regarded as remuneration of the Brokers and/or Agents for placing the Insurance.

In the event of any occurrence likely to result in a claim under this Policy IMMEDIATE NOTICE should be given to Edward Lumley & Sons (S) Pte. Ltd., P.O. Box 111, Singapore.

W

E. & O. E.

Insured with Underwriters at LLOYD'S LONDON

in Hongkong	currency	
Rate		........%
Premium	HK	$ 15,444.35
Policy & Stamp		$ ----
	HK	$ 15,444.35

For Edward Lumley & Sons (Singapore) Pte. Ltd.
as BROKERS

Manager.

Lee's Lloyds of London policy

K

LLOYD'S ACCIDENT POLICY

Whereas the Assured with a view to effecting an insurance as hereinafter defined with Us who have hereunto subscribed our Names (hereinafter call "the Underwriters") has made a written proposal which proposal together with any statements, warranties or declarations contained therein shall be deemed to be incorporated herein and to form the basis of this contract and has paid to Us a premium for the first period of insurance, the receipt of which premium is hereby acknowledged.

And Whereas the name, address and occupation of the said Assured, the date of the written proposal and the amount of the premium for the first period of insurance are specified overleaf, together with the geographical limits and the period or periods within which this Policy shall remain in effect,

WE THE UNDERWRITERS hereby agree with the Assured, to the extent and in the manner herein provided, that if the Assured sustains bodily injury as herein defined we will pay, to the Assured, or to the Assured's Executors or Administrators, according to the Schedule of Compensation overleaf within Seven Days after the total claim shall be substantiated under this Policy,

PROVIDED ALWAYS THAT:—

1. (a) Compensation shall not be payable under more than one of the items of the Schedule of Compensation in respect of the consequences of one accident, except for any compensation payable hereunder in respect of temporary partial disablement preceding or following temporary total disablement, and
   (b) No weekly compensation shall become payable until the total amount thereof has been ascertained and agreed.
   If, nevertheless, payment be made for weekly compensation, the amount so paid shall be deducted from any lump sum becoming claimable in respect of the same accident.
2. The total sum payable under this Policy in respect of any one or more accidents shall not exceed in all in any one period of insurance the largest sum insured under any one of the items contained in the Schedule of Compensation or added to this Policy by endorsement, except that the Underwriters will in addition pay Medical Expenses as herein provided.
3. If Item No. 1 of the Schedule of Compensation is not covered then no claim shall by payable, other than for weekly compensation and medical expenses, in respect of any accident which would have given rise to a claim under Item No. 1 has that item been covered.

DEFINITIONS

In this Policy:—

1. "BODILY INJURY" means bodily injury which
   (a) is sustained by the Assured during the period of this Policy.
   (b) is caused by an accident, and
   (c) solely and independently of any other cause, except illness directly resulting from, or medical or surgical treatment rendered necessary by, such injury, occasions the death or disablement of the Assured within twelve calendar months from the date of the accident by which such injury is caused.
2. "ACCIDENT" includes exposure resulting from a mishap to an aircraft or vessel in which the Assured is travelling.
3. "TOTAL DISABLEMENT" means disablement which entirely prevents the Assured from attending to his business or occupation (of any and every kind) or if he has no business or occupation from attending to his usual duties.
4. "PARTIAL DISABLEMENT" means disablement which prevents the Assured from attending to a substantial part of his business or occupation, or if he has no business or occupation from attending to a substantial part of his duties.
5. "PERMANENT" means lasting twelve calendar months and at the expiry of that period being beyond hope of improvement.
6. "LOSS OF LIMB" means loss by physical separation of a hand at or above the wrist or of a foot at or above the ankle.
7. "MEDICAL EXPENSES" means expenses properly incurred by the Assured for medical, surgical, manipulative, massage, therapeutic, X-ray or nursing treatment, including the cost of medical supplies and ambulance hire, but excluding the cost of board and lodging.
8. "AIR TRAVEL" means being in or on or boarding an aircraft for the purpose of flying therein or alighting therefrom following a flight.
9. Words in the masculine gender shall include the feminine.

EXCLUSIONS

This Policy does not cover death or disablement

1. consequent on war, invasion or civil war;
2. consequent on the Assured engaging in or taking part in
   (a) naval, military or air force service or operations.
   (b) winter sports outside Great Britain, Northern Ireland, the Isle of Man, the Channel Islands or the Republic of Ireland,
   (c) driving or riding motor cycles or motor scooters over 125 c.c.
   (d) hunting, or driving or riding in any kind of race;
3. directly or indirectly consequent on the Assured engaging in air travel, except as a passenger in any properly licensed aircraft being operated by a licensed airline in accordance with published schedules of flights or timetables or in a properly licensed multi-engined aircraft being operated by any other licensed commercial air carrier;

Chapter Twelve

Lee's Lloyds of London policy

4. resulting from suicide or attempted suicide or intentional self-injury, or from deliberate exposure to exceptional danger (except in an attempt to save human life), or from the Assured's own criminal act, or sustained whilst the Assured is in a state of insanity

CONDITIONS

1. If the Assured shall engage in any occupation in which greater risks may be incurred than in the occupation disclosed in this Policy without first notifying the Underwriters and obtaining their written agreement to the amendment of the Policy (subject to the payment of such reasonable additional premium as the Underwriters may require as the consideration for such agreement) then no claim shall be payable in respect of any accident arising out of or in the course of such occupation.

2. Immediate notice must be given to the Underwriters of any accident which causes or may cause disablement within the meaning of this Policy, and the Assured must as early as possible place himself under the care of a duly qualified practitioner.

Immediate notice must be given to the Underwriters in the event of death of the Assured resulting or alleged to result from an accident.

In no case will the Underwriters be liable to pay compensation to the Assured or his representatives unless the medical adviser or advisers appointed by the Underwriters for the purpose shall be allowed so often as may be deemed necessary to make an examination of the person of the Assured.

3. Any fraud, mis-statement or concealment either in the proposal on which this insurance is based or in relation to any other matter affecting this insurance or in connection with the making of any claim hereunder shall render this Policy null and void and all claims hereunder shall be forfeited.

NOW KNOW YE that We, the Underwriters, Members of Syndicate(s) whose definitive Number(s) in the attached list are set out in the Table over-leaf, or attached overleaf, hereby bind Ourselves, each for his own part and not one for another, our respective Heirs, Executors and Administrators, and each of us in respect of his due proportion only, to pay in respect of claims which shall be substantiated under this Policy, in the proportions ascertained by reference to the attached list the Amount, Percentage or Proportion of the total liability under this Policy which is in the said Table set opposite the definitive Number of the Syndicate of which such Underwriter is a member.

IN WITNESS whereof the Manager of Lloyd's Policy Signing Office has subscribed his Name on behalf of each of Us.

The Policy No. is ZHA.3/145/0002-ZHA.3/PA/0001	
The Assured is Mr. Bruce Lee,	
The address of the Assured is	(AS OVER)
The occupation of the Assured is that of Film Maker	
The date of the written proposal is 3.5.73	The premium for the first period of insurance is HK$15,444.35
The geographical limits of this Policy are—anywhere in the World.	
The period of insurance is from 30.4.73 to 30.4.74 ~~both days inclusive~~ and for such further period or periods as may be mutually agreed upon.	

Dated in Singapore the 15.5.73

SCHEDULE OF COMPENSATION

This Policy insures in respect only of such of the following benefits as have an amount (or a percentage of the Capital Sum Insured) inserted against them.

1.	Death ...	100%
2.	Permanent total loss of sight of both eyes ...	100%
3.	Permanent total loss of sight of one eye ...	100%
4.	Loss of two Limbs ...	100%
5.	Loss of one Limb ...	100%
6.	Permanent total loss of sight of one eye and loss of one limb ...	100%
7.	Permanent total disablement (other than loss of sight of one or both eyes or loss of limb) ...	100%
8.	Temporary total disablement ...	Not Covered Per week
9.	Temporary partial disablement ...	Not Covered Per week

(items 8 and 9) so long as such disablement continues but not exceeding altogether ----- consecutive weeks for any single disablement.

MEDICAL EXPENSES:— Medical Expenses will in addition be paid by the Underwriters up to but not exceeding 15 per cent. of the total amount of any claim admitted under items 8 or 9.

N.B. — All benefits which are not insured are to be completed by the insertion of the words "Not Covered".

NMA 1089
18.12.58

Fourth, Lee was insured for similar perils under the AIA policy, thereby placing himself into double indemnity. And fifth, and most discrediting of all, Lee had a habit of using marijuana.

In consultation with a team of attorneys, Adrian Marshall went to work in a frantic attempt to unravel this mess, only to find himself on the defensive. Marshall seemed to ask all the wrong questions. He had a way of doing that. Who exactly had ordered all this life insurance? IN reading the application form, it appeared that Bruce was unaware of the existence of the AIA policy when he was asked to fill out the application to Lloyds of London. After a thorough investigation, Marshall noted that it appeared that Raymond Chow might have been the one who ordered the AIA policy. Did this mean that Chow was responsible for the double indemnity? And whose idea was the $1.5-million? On the initial proposal form both the date and amount of insurance were missing. Why was this? And had anyone at Lloyds mentioned the nonpayment clause for death resulting from the insured's own criminal act? It had been ruled that Bruce had died from taking Equagesic, which was a prescription drug to which he did not have a prescription. Could this have been viewed as a criminal act? Lloyds hadn't mentioned it. Perhaps they hadn't even seen it.

Most peculiar of all, there was no record anywhere showing who exactly had paid for the first premium of HK$15,444 (US$3,285) on the Lloyds policy. Clearly Bruce hadn't paid it. Upon delving further into the matter, Marshall discovered that no one had paid it!

Following three days of panic, Marshall came upon a fine-line technicality in the policy, which stated that the insured had paid or agreed to pay the initial premium. Subsequently, the premium was promptly submitted to Lloyds through Lo Yuen Enterprises. Although Lloyds had offered to refund the total premium amount as full compensation, this ludicrous offer was rejected by Adrian and Linda.

Financed by the moneys received from the sale of the Cumberland house, Marshall entered into his second year of negotiations with the Lloyds solicitors. Following weeks of heated legal fencing, the Lloyds defense (and subsequently the defense of AIA, who were now in double-harness with Lloyds) boiled down to two main issues. First, Bruce's unreported back injury and, second, the matter of Lee's illicit drug use.

The medical facts surrounding Bruce's 1970 back problem were made readily available, and within days the attorneys for Lloyds and AIA backpedaled, for it was clear that, owing to the inconsequential nature of the injury, there was no reason for Bruce to have mentioned it.

That aside, the focus now centered on drugs. The issue had nothing to do with whether Bruce had died of ingesting marijuana, but that he had not disclosed his use of the drug when he applied for the insurance. Attorneys for Lloyds quoted from the policy: "Condition 3 of the Policy stipulates that any misstatement or concealment in the Proposal Form on which the Policy is based shall render the policy null and void, and all claims thereunder shall be forfeited."

The question was simple: Had Bruce been in the habit of using marijuana before May 3, 1973 when he signed the proposal form? Well over a million dollars was riding on this simple yes or no answer.

Realistically, the question had nothing to do with Bruce's use of marijuana before May 1973, for there were scores of individuals who knew that Bruce had been using marijuana for years and that he even had his own water pipe collection.

Had this information fell into the camp of the Lloyds/AIA defense attorneys, a huge red flag would have resulted, for it was common knowledge that, in addition to opium, #3 heroin has for decades been smoked throughout Asia via a water pipe. As a matter of record, as of October 1989, Linda Lee still owned Bruce's water pipe and drug paraphernalia collection. Unlike most of his personal possessions, it escaped the several public auction blocks that netted Linda nearly a half million dollars.

Besides Bruce's reputation of using marijuana, it was known to many that Linda had been baking marijuana brownies for Bruce, and others, on the set of Enter the Dragon. Therefore, the real issue, as far as Linda and Adrian were concerned, was not whether Bruce had used marijuana before May 1973, but could Lloyds prove it.

Perhaps most damaging was the July 24, 1974 sworn deposition of Dr. Harold Karpman. According to Karpman's notes, Bruce had admitted to smoking between six to ten marijuana cigarettes daily. Since Karpman had examined Bruce on May 25, 1973, this meant that if Bruce had not smoked marijuana prior to May 3, he would have developed a daily six to ten marijuana cigarette habit in just over two weeks. This was hardly believable.

Although Linda Lee was not ready to confirm her husband's use of marijuana prior to May 3, she had no

Lee's Lloyds of London policy receipt

Debit to

SHORWARD UNDERWRITERS, LTD.

1114-1116 PRINCE'S BUILDING
10, CHATER ROAD, HONG KONG
TEL. H-229630 H-241001-3
TELEGRAMS: "APLINS"

凱風保險有限公司

Debit № L-4606

Messrs. Mr. Bruce Lee

Date 24th May 1973

To	Premium under Lloyd's Personal Accident No. ZHA.3/145/0002- ZHA.3/PA/0001 ...	HK$15,444.35	
	30th April 73 to 30th April 74 — 7%	1,081.10	HK$ 14,363.25

KINDLY SEND YOUR CROSSED CHEQUE TO THE ABOVE ADDRESS

choice but to admit to her knowledge of his use of marijuana after that date. Having become a rather hesitant and halting witness, she alleged that such use was kept at a bare minimum, stating for the record that "because of Bruce's professional need to keep fit, he would not be foolish to use marijuana more than just occasionally."

Upon completion of their discovery phase, the attorneys representing AIA declared that, in addition to other things, they had an investigation report of a witness interview in which said witness stated personal knowledge of Bruce's marijuana use for three to four years before his death. Apparently, somewhere, someone had talked and was willing to take the stand.

After three years of negotiations, the estate and the insurance companies had reached an impasse and were head ed to court. As often happens in such matters, the insurance companies weighed the cost of litigation against the cost of settlement and ultimately opted for the latter.

As to the million-dollar policy with Lloyds of London, in return for a quick filing of Notification of Discontinuance, the company offered the estate the sum of US$129,000, which was a mere pittance of the policy's face value, and Adrian Marshall accepted.

In the matter of the AIA policy, the company settled for half the policy's face value and wrote a check to the estate for US$100,000. Curiously, when the check arrived it was divided, with $75,000 being sent to Adrian Marshall, and the balance of $25,000 being paid to, of all people, Raymond Chow.

CHAPTER 13

The Settlement

The funds that Linda and Adrian received in August 1974 from the sale of 41Cumberland Road helped considerably to finance their ongoing war with Raymond Chow and his dream team. A year had passed since the initial volleys, and with the worldwide release of Enter the Dragon having resulted in sky-rocketing box-office figures, clearly Chow owed Linda and Adrian something, and he had no choice but to come to the bargaining table.

At a meting in Hong Kong with estate attorneys Brian Tisdall, Raymond Chow finally acknowledged owing Bruce, in addition to a US$3,000 bonus for The Big Boss and a second bonus of US$50,000 for Fist of Fury, US$75,000 as a director's emolument for The Way of the Dragon, and, by virtue of several more, previously undisclosed oral agreements: (1) 50 percent of the net earnings of The Way of the Dragon (reportedly US$2,000,000, and (2) 5 percent of the net profits of Fists of Fury from Golden Harvest and another 5 percent from Chow personally.

Following his disclosures to Tisdall, Chow agreed to

prepare a statement of the financial account of The Way of the Dragon and to send the net sum owing to the estate to Johnson, Stokes, and Masters. The following day, however, Chow advised Tisdall that he had discovered, upon reexamining the books of Golden Harvest, that the total earnings of The Way of the Dragon had been included in the books of Concord. This meant that it would be premature for Chow to send any money over the JSM, because no one had yet decided how to resolve the matter of dividing Concord Productions Ltd. In plain and simple language, this meant that the stall continued, and they money would remain in Chow's bank accounts.

Following a meeting between the representatives of the estate and Raymond Chow, J.B. Osborne contacted Adrian Marshall's law partner, Bryant Burton. As far as Osborne was concerned, Chow and his attorneys were dolling out scraps of information one tiny morsel at a time. As to Adrian's numerous requests for a full audit of both Golden Harvest and Concord, they continued to fall upon deaf ears.

Days later the matter became even more convoluted. Regarding the two bonuses and the director's emolument owed to Bruce totaling US$155,000, Chow no suddenly recalled that not only had Bruce already been paid, but in fact he had been overpaid and, as a result, the Bruce Lee Estate owned Chow US$75,000. It all had to do with a credit for US$85,000 made a year or two before on the Golden Harvest books in Bruce's name. Was this somehow to be confused with the US$4,000 monthly living expense paid to the Lees, in addition to the US$64,000 for remodeling made to 41 Cumberland Road, all of which had been allegedly debited to what was clearly a slush account? Chow wasn't sure.

The IRS wasn't sure either, although they were keenly interested. More problems to be worked out by more and more expensive attorneys and accountants.

Not long into Chow's power ploy, there surfaced one underrated player—Warner Brothers, whose studio executives couldn't be controlled by Raymond Chow. Contractually Warner's had agreed to pay Bruce US$100,000 for his work on Enter the Dragon, and now that the picture was finished, Warner's owed Bruce, or his estate, another US$75,000.

Closer to the Hong Kong homefront, attorney Marshall tossed his first noose at Chow's head. After talking with Marshall in September 1974, J.B. Osborne from Peat, Marwick, Mitchell & Co. received a letter from Bob Miller at their Los Angeles office. Regarding Concord, the instructions could not have been clearer. The most imperative thing the attorneys had to accomplish, if they accomplished nothing else, was to obtain a signed agreement that would put an immediate stop to the transmitting abroad of Warner Brothers' moneys, or at least the estate's 50 percent, into Raymond Chow's offshore bank accounts.

Concurrently, the attorneys for the estate wasted no time in stating their position as to the past business agreements between Bruce Lee and Raymond Chow. Fundamentally, they did not believe that the agreement of May 30, 1972 between Golden Harvest and Concord Productions had any teeth, arguing that the agreement was superseded by the contract between Warner Brothers, Concord, and Sequoia dated November 3, 1972, which was also signed by Golden Harvest by Raymond Chow, president, guaranteeing the performance of all of Concord's obligations. In lay terms this meant that the Estate of Bruce Lee had got into bed with the almighty Warner Brothers and that Raymond Chow would have to perform according to the terms and conditions of this considerably more binding contract that had the teeth of a great white.

Sitting on the sidelines was also the matter of the raw fight footage of Bruce Lee in battle with Kareem Abdul-Jabbar, hapkido master Ji Han Jai, and Dan Inosanto. In November 1972, nearly eight months before Lee's death, the footage had been placed in the cold storage vaults at Golden Harvest. With Warner Brothers and Concord Productions having struck a bonanza with Enter the Dragon, this only remaining unseen footage of Bruce could presumably be worth a fortune. Surely Linda Lee knew of its existence, but did she know who legally owned it?

In July 1974 Adrian Marshal wanted Raymond to redeem all of the estate's holdings in Concord stock for an undivided 50.001 percent interest in Enter the Dragon and The Way of the Dragon, which would result in Warner Brothers sending all royalties directly to the estate, by that bypassing Raymond Chow. Although Marshall felt that a cash sellout would be in his and Linda's best interest and quickly began to negotiate a figure in excess of US$3,000,000, Linda's legal arm in Hong Kong had grown impatient with Chow's stalling and now emphatically demanded an audit of his books. Osborne's main concern was that he had become convinced that Chow was now using Concord funds to finance Golden Harvest film projects, but without an audit he couldn't prove it.

Inevitably too much pressure had been brought to bear on Raymond Chow, and on August 6, 1975, just a few days short of two years following Bruce Lee's death, he made the following buyout offer to Adrian Marshall:

Enter the Dragon
(Warner Bros.) . . . . .US$3,816,276

The Way of the Dragon

(1) South-east Asia 1973 179,036
(2) South-east Asia 1974 200,000
(3) Bryanston 328,280
(4) US – Other 450,000
Subtotal $5,344,392

Game of Death (unfinished) 200,000

Subtotal $5,544,392

Future residuals 250,000
Gross value (US) $5,794,392

Less: Legal fees 30,000

Hong Kong taxes 952,000

Net Value $4,812,392

Linda Lee's 50% interest . . . . .US$2,400,000

Chapter Thirteen

Although Marshall was troubled by the fact that he knew that Chow's books had been done after Bruce's death, he had no choice but to accept Chow's figures, and he countered the offer at US$2,700,000, in addition to the release of all other estate indebtedness to Raymond Chow and Golden Harvest, the total of which Marshall estimated at US$300,000.

In an odd twist of events, in January 1976 when Linda's Concord stock was officially sold to Raymond for US$2,700,000, the balance sheet of Bruce's corporation, Lo Yuen, on 3/31/75 had shown HK$652,131 owed to Concord. Curiously, Raymond Chow gratuitously forgave this indebtedness. Moreover, around that same time it was determined that Lo Yuen owed an additional HK$20,000 to Raymond, which he also forgave.

Linda's accountant over at PMM&CO was instantly alarmed and contacted Adrian Marshall and warned him that Linda should not acknowledge the validity of any financial statement she may later regret. The problem was that the published balance sheet, which would inevitably land on the desk of the IRS, had not shown any record of Raymond Chow's forgiveness of these debts.

There had been other enormous tax problems. In the eyes of Linda's Hong Kong accountants, they suspected that Raymond Chow had used a tax figure that was far too excessive when it applied the HK profits tax rate of approximately 16.5 percent to Concord's worldwide income when it should have been applied only to Concord's HK source income. Their suspicions were subsequently confirmed.

Raymond Chow was insulted and instantly wrote a sizzling letter to Richard Mark, stating that he was furious that, due to such meddling, Concord now had to pay a sizeable tax. And that wasn't all. Chow further blasted Peat, Marwick, Mitchell & Co. for doing a sloppy job in setting up the books and overseas accounts of Concord.

Richard Heller discussed Chow's innuendo with Brian Osborne and learned that (1) PMM&CO did not set up the books and records of Concord. The books had been set up well before Bruce Lee's death and any PMM&CO local involvement in the affairs of Concord. According to Brian Osborne, Raymond should have formed an offshore company to capture the non-Hong Kong film rental income. By the time PMM&CO in Hong Kong became involved, it was too late to form an offshore company; (2) There was nothing in the Hong Kong revenue law that exempted all foreign source film income. If PMM&CO was correct, apparently 50 percent was subject to Hong Kong taxation (which the use of an offshore corporation at the onset could have avoided), and (3) PMM&CO's financial statements for Concord for the year ending March 31, 1974 reflected the following:

Net profits before taxes	HK$6,390,634
LESS: provision for taxation	725,000
Net profits after taxes	HK$5,665,634
	US$993,000

They further stated that the effective tax rate was 11.3 percent, after having taken into account a partial exemption of foreign source income. Thus, in their opinion, any reader of the PMM&CO prepared Concord financial statements could easily have seen the existence of some

Hong Kong tax liability. According to Brian Tisdall, Raymond Chow knew that Hong Kong Inland Revenue may have rejected a "no tax on foreign income" position and for that very reason he (Brian) had insisted upon a full tax provision in the Concord financial statements. The matter was still being negotiated with Inland Revenue.

From the above, to PMM&CO it appeared that if one were looking solely to U.S. source income for Concord valuation purposes, the effective rate of tax should have been about 11.25 percent. This assumed that half of the profits were non-Hong Kong source and were therefore subject to only one-half the normal Hong Kong tax rate. Whether this was reasonable, they did not know. But it did approximate the effective tax provision rate.

Paramount to all else, what stand out in the past several pages is the enormous amount of money that was floating around Bruce Lee at the time of his death. And the operative word here is "floating," because it is hard to believe that Bruce, who was often in a drugged state and in a questionable frame of mind (including bouts of amnesia), had much of a handle on any of it, let alone a workable understanding of the financial complexities.

Perhaps most important of all is that this sizeable fortune was tied to nothing more than what Adrian Marshall had initially referred to as "oral, virtually unenforceable agreements between Bruce Lee and Raymond Chow." Perhaps initially Raymond Chow saw it that way as well.

CHAPTER 14

Quiet on the Set

To the press Wu Ngan became known as Lee's butler, perhaps because it was felt that no mystery of this magnitude would be complete without someone alleging that "the butler did it." In this particular case the scenario wasn't "Mr. Green in the Library with the Knife," but Wu Ngan in the Kitchen with Poison." Motive? Several industrious press hounds had uncovered what they avowed was highly incriminating evidence. According to The Star, practically everything Lee owned was in his servant's name, including his house, his phone, and 80 percent of his stock in Concord. What was this all about, the press demanded? What secret did Lee's servant have over him?

According to Wu, Bruce had done this so that people could not find out where he lived. Really? Bruce Lee wasn't Howard Hughes with a fake beard and mustache sneaking around Death Valley in a '52 faded Plymouth. Bruce drove all over Hong Kong in his convertible Mercedes wearing a white three-piece Brioni suit. What's more, within hours of Lee's death, 41 Cumberland Road was besieged with fans and reporters who knew exactly where Bruce lived, not to mention every kid in the neighborhood who had known for a year where the Lee children parked their bikes.

When questioned by reporters about his massive good fortune, Mr.Wu said simply, "He trusted me," before retreating behind the locked iron gates of the Cumberland residence. It was a pathetically weak answer, for in the final months of his life, Bruce had become well known as a man who trusted no one.

Did Wu Ngan kill Bruce in an effort to obtain Lee's home, as some have alleged? Technically Bruce Lee did not hold title to 41 Cumberland Road. Title was held by Lo Yuen Enterprises, Ltd. The real question, however, is whether Wu Ngan actually knew this, or was he under another assumption? In either case, although according to corporate records Wu Ngan was a shareholder and one of the directors of Lo Yuen, when the house was sold for cash in August 1974, the entire proceeds went unchallenged to Linda Lee.

If the allegation that Wu Ngan murdered his boss to gain Bruce Lee's controlling interest in Concord Productions is true, there are several high hurdles to get over. To begin with, Raymond Chow is too keen a businessman to have allowed the possibility of finding himself in business with Wu Ngan, should something have happened to Bruce. That is to say, imagine Chow's explanation to the press: "Good morning, ladies and gentlemen, let me again express my deepest sorrow over the passing of my previous associate Bruce Lee and, while you're here, let me introduce my new business partner, Mr. Lee's house servant." It's absurd. Secondly, it is difficult to envision any corporate law firm allowing such an arrangement. And finally, at the time of Lee's death, Enter the Dragon had not yet premiered and, as a result, Concord Productions wasn't worth much. Again, the presumption is that Wu Ngan was thinking along this line, which, of course, may not have been the case.

In any event, one could argue that unless Bruce had taken in a complete moron, Wu Ngan had far more to gain had Bruce remained alive. On the other hand, Bruce was leaving Hong Kong. Permanently, according to his own words. Had he planned on taking the Wu family with him, which would have meant sponsoring their immigration? Questions. Unending questions.

Although it seems doubtful that Bruce would have legally placed his home and stock holdings in his servant's name, it is entirely possible that a similar arrangement had been proposed for some time. The reason centers on the escalating possibility of Bruce Lee being sued as a result of his increasing and unpredictable acts of violence. In this regard, if Lee's assets, what little he had at the time, were in the name of Wu Ngan, it was more likely restricted to the degree that title transfer was in the form of a legal document tucked away in some lawyer's desk, waiting in the wings if needed.

Does this mean that Wu Ngan is clean? If he is, then one must as the obvious question which is simply: "Where is Wu Ngan?" Why haven't we heard from this Far Eastern clone of G. Gordon Liddy for nearly three decades? In addition to documentary films, tributes and a televised A&E hour-long biography, hundreds of articles and several book biographies have been written. Add to that literally countless personal interviews that have been conducted with those

The personal loan from Linda Lee to Wu Ngan

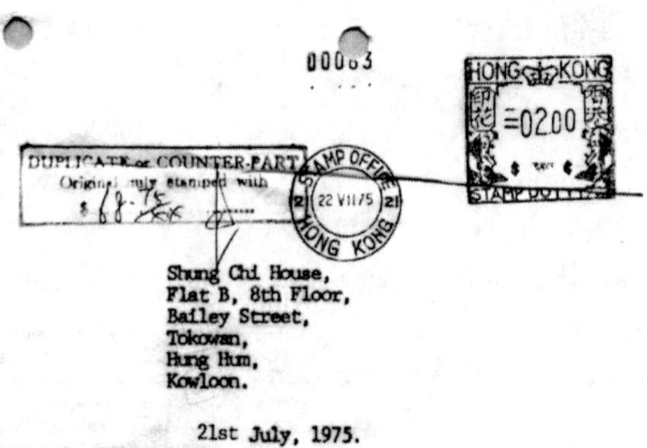

00003

HONG KONG

=02.00

STAMP DUTY

DUPLICATE or COUNTER-PART
Original duly stamped with
$ 68.75

STAMP OFFICE
22 VII 75
HONG KONG

Shung Chi House,
Flat B, 8th Floor,
Bailey Street,
Tokowan,
Hung Hum,
Kowloon.

21st July, 1975.

ON DEMAND I PROMISE to pay to LINDA EMERY LEE or order the sum of United States Dollars Fifty Five Thousand (US$55,000:00) together with interest thereon at the rate of eight per cent (8%) per annum from the date hereof together with all expenses and costs incurred in connection with the making or enforcement of this Promissory Note.

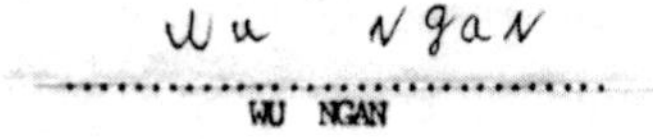

Wu Ngan

WU NGAN

who knew Bruce Lee. On a more personal level, nearly a half-million dollars has been generated from Linda's public auctioning of Bruce's personal possessions. And in 1993 the feature-length life story of Bruce Lee, Dragon, was released by MCA Universal.

At the time of his death, Bruce had very little money,

and Wu Ngan must have had considerably less or he wouldn't be the servant. So why haven't we heard from the man who not only lived with Bruce as a child and appeared with him in his movies and on Hong Kong television, but also lived with him during the adult years when Bruce Lee became a national hero? There was money to be made here. Why hasn't Mr. Wu cashed in on his share? Maybe he already did and just didn't tell anyone.

Perhaps the answer lies in the payment of US$55,000 (in 1968 equal to the full purchase prince of Lee's Bel Air home and in 2002 the equivalent to over US$400,000!) in the form of a personal loan from Linda Lee to Wu Ngan a short time after Bruce died. The note was drafted by the Hong Kong attorneys for the Estate of Bruce Lee and earmarked for use at a future date. A year later, upon Linda Lee's acquisition of the money, the note was signed on July 21, 1975 and then recorded the following morning. Although there was never a date listed as to when the note would become due, the interest rate was 8 percent together with expenses and costs incurred in connection with the drafting or enforcement of the note.

When a year later the Inland Island Revenue (Hong Kong's version of the IRS) billed Linda Lee for the interest she would have received from Wu Ngan on the above referenced note, she responded by stating that she had not received any money from Mr. Wu and then promptly amended the note's interest rate to zero.

What is highly disturbing about this entire matter is that during this period, Linda was having a difficult time qualifying for an American Express card and bank loan, and was living on the financial edge due to her ongoing war with

Chapter Fourteen

The personal loan from Linda Lee to Robert Baker

GOLDEN HARVEST (INT) LIMITED
嘉禾機構有限公司
8 HAMMER HILL ROAD
KOWLOON HONG KONG
TEL. K-250136-9
CABLE ADD. 'GOLDENSUN'
香港九龍斧山道八號

I hereby acknowledge that I have received the amount of HK$10,000.00 (HONGKONG DOLLARS TEN THOUSAND ONLY) from Golden Harvest on behalf of Linda Lee of Concord Productions. I agree to repay the above amount to Mrs. Linda Lee in Seattle, Washington.

Robert Baker
Robert Baker
January 7, 1974.

André Morgan
Jan. 7th 1974

Linda,
Gave Bob. the money today, he said he will see to pay back the money. Take care!
Andre

Raymond Chow. At its best case scenario, this entire matter just smacks of criminal extortion. Curiously this was also around the time that both Lloyds of London and AIA began hinting about the existence of a star witness they claimed had knowledge of Bruce's three to four year use of marijuana.

On the other hand, Wu Ngan wasn't the only one who knew about Bruce's long-standing drug use. Maybe this all had to do with what went on at Cumberland Road the day Bruce died. Perhaps Wu Ngan was at the house. Maybe he heard something. Or saw something. Aside from the afternoon of July 20, 1973, surely he had knowledge of what had gone on behind those stone walls, both before and after Bruce Lee's death. Undoubtedly the mysterious Wu Ngan had countless stories to tell. Then again, perhaps Wu Ngan was operating as a go-between? It's a curious sum, isn't it? Fifty-five thousand? Fifty thousand is a much tidier principal figure, with the additional $5,000 as a tidy 10 percent fee?

For the record, based on an extensive worldwide investigative search for Wu Ngan, for all intents and purposes it would appear that Lee's mysterious butler has long since vanished into thin air. And, no, not one cent of the "loan" was ever repaid.

The elusive Wu Ngan wasn't the only player to have suddenly departed Hong Kong in the wake of Bruce's death. In fact, Bobby Baker may well have taken the same flight. You remember Baker, lee's international gofer slash bodyguard. One can only imagine what Baker may have known. As fate would have it, he was in Hong Kong on the day Bruce died. And like Wu, Baker "borrowed" money from

Linda Lee on his way out of town. HK$10,000 to be exact, advanced to him by Linda in the form of a personal loan.

Only with Baker, there was no one year waiting period as there was with Wu Ngan, and Linda was forced to plead for the money from Raymond Chow within days of her husband's death. Again, for the record, Baker never paid back one nickel of the loan, and like Wu Ngan, Linda never heard from him again.

The years following Lee's death took their toll on Baker, who became an alcoholic recluse who would escape further into the bottle when questioned about his past relationship with Bruce. Bobby Baker died in Stockton in 1992 at the young age of 52 of cirrhosis of the liver.

Ultimately, with the money received from the sale of 41 Cumberland Road, the insurance settlements, and Raymond Chow, things began to turn around for Linda, and she soon left Seattle and moved to the upscale community of Rolling Hills Estates in southern California, ironically just a stone's throw from the family home of Adrian Marshall. What a small world. When questioned as to the reasons for the move, Linda smiled thoughtfully, then replied that she had "missed the southern sunshine."

CHAPTER 15

The Estate of Bruce Lee

"When I die, these guys will probably do something that I won't like. They'll probably build monuments, have impressive creeds, hang pictures of me in the halls, and bow to me."

• Bruce Lee

Although Bruce Lee died physically on July 20, 1973, he has lived for the past twenty-nine years as the legal embodiment known as the Estate of Bruce Lee. This book would be incomplete without a general examination of these years over which a man and his beloved and personal martial art have become a worldwide corporate industry.

Prior to the release of Enter the Dragon, Bruce Lee had for the most part removed himself from the martial arts community. His three schools had closed, and he wasn't teaching any longer, either publicly or privately. In the United States, aside from the small segment of the population who had viewed Lee's three Golden Harvest/Concord releases, most people remembered Bruce as The Green Hornet's sidekick Kato. Around the time of Bruce's death, to the martial arts community at large, the real warriors of that era were Joe Lewis, Chuck Norris, Mike Stone, and a good many other dedicated martial artists who were toughing it out on the tournament circuit and teaching the masses. That was a Friday. The following Monday, after the weekend release of Enter the Dragon's eleven minutes of Lee's swashbuckling fight footage, Bruce Lee soon became the master of masters, the final word on everything from the horse stance to metaphysical matters for the next twenty-nine years. Just how did that happen?

The answer is simple. At the time Bruce Lee died, the world knew next to nothing about him. To illustrate, one only need glance at the skeletal bibliography contained in the first biographical work ever written on Lee called The Legend of Bruce Lee (A Dell Book, 1974) by Alex Ben Block. Essentially Block had nothing to draw from except general reference material such as John Chen's 1001 Chinese Sayings, Y.T. Kwong's Chinese Proverbs, Lao Tzu's Way of Life, and Raymond Van Over's Chinese Mystics.

The fact that there was little known of Bruce Lee's life from the cradle to the grave sent the hungry media racing to the doorstep of the one person who could most expeditiously fill in all the blanks—Linda Lee. Unquestionably this lack of information on Bruce Lee presented Linda with an ideal photo opportunity to essentially create her own legend of her deceased husband. From the beginning, however, Linda Lee by no means acted alone.

Practically speaking, upon the death of Bruce Lee, attorney Adrian Marshall became lord and master of the Lee empire. As soon as was legally possible, not only did Linda bestow upon Adrian the title of the estate's attorney, but she also designated him as the worldwide exclusive merchandising agent for the name and likeness of her deceased husband. Marshall held this position until the summer of 1988 when he and Linda sold most of their merchandising rights to the new lord and master MCA Universal. For those who are unfamiliar with the abbreviation, the letters M-C-A stand for Merchandising Corporation of America.

Following the death of Bruce Lee, Adrian Marshall became obsessed with doggedly pursuing anyone and everyone who demonstrated an interest, legitimate or otherwise, in making a dollar, yen, lire, rupee, pound sterling, or tribal bead from anything having to do with Bruce Lee. As a result, regardless of whether obtained from outside enterprise or in-house marketing, Linda and Adrian amassed a fortune from the Madison Avenue style commercialization of Bruce Lee in the form of T-shirts, video games, cassette deals, children's trading cards, patches, emblems, syndicated comic strip projects, uniforms, precious metal medallions, public auctions of Bruce's personal belongings, numerous magazine articles and book projects, several low-budget movie rip-offs, and residuals and royalties from MCA Universal's release of Dragon. In the mid-1990s word from the Lee camp foretold of an upcoming Bruce Lee encyclopedia, a day-by-day, minute-to-minute accounting of the master's life in book form for under a hundred dollars.

Speaking as the successor to Bruce Lee's Jeet Kune Do Society and echoing the sentiments of a large sector of the martial arts community, Bruce Lee's protégé Dan Inosanto bitterly stated in 1976: "The Jeet Kune Do organi zation has purposely maintained a low profile, wanting no part of the burgeoning Bruce Lee market that has nothing whatsoever to do with the man or his art."

Perhaps such commercialization would have been far less objectionable had Linda and Adrian limited their ambitions to Bruce's film image and not tampered with his personal martial art of Jeet Kune Do. This, however, was not the case.

You will recall in the introduction mention of Bruce Lee's legendary six black journals. Over a period of about three years, during the late 1960s, Bruce had taken to writing in these journals. This writing was not original, however. Instead, Bruce was merely copying specific sections from many of the several hundred books he had amassed on the various fighting arts, both eastern and western. Essentially these journals were to be used as Bruce's personal and private source material, and he never had any intention of publishing their content.

After Bruce died, however, Linda and Adrian agreed to have published, by expanding on the extremely limited contents of these journals (over 90 percent of the journal's pages were blank), what became <u>The Tao of Jeet Kune Do</u>, alleging that the book contained the deep personal wisdom of the master himself. This, incidentally, is the same text that is vividly showcased in MCA Universal's Dragon. The ideas put forth in the movie are that, first, Bruce personally dictated the book to Linda while he was hospitalized with his crippling back injury and, second, that the book was published while Bruce was alive. Both totally false.

Initially when the book was published, Jesse Glover was the first to issue a formal complaint in his book, <u>Bruce</u>

Lee: "The Tao of Jeet Kune Do is at best a poor joke on a great martial artist ... There is little in the book that will help a beginner develop basic skills, and much of the text is open to broad interpretation. The best that can be said about the book is that it isn't a book written by Bruce, but rather a poor interpretation of his notes."

According to Joe Snyder, who has taken it upon himself to track down the real authors of the book, Bruce Lee had copied verbatim into his journals passages totaling approximately 13,019 words, together with twenty-three tracing of illustrations, extracted from seventeen works of others!

Presently in its twentieth printing and offered in nine languages, The Tao of Jeet Kune Do, for well over a decade a bestseller, has lined the pockets of a few at the expense of misleading countless martial artists of all ages and levels of proficiency. Hopefully the day will come when the great masters whose writings are contained in The Tao of Jeet Kune Do will be honored, both in print and monetarily, for their work that has for too many years been wrongly and purposely credited to Bruce Lee. Perhaps the worst example of plagiarism occurred in 2000 when the estate's author, John Little, wrongly attributed to Bruce Lee the writing ("The Passionate State of Mind") of renowned philosopher (and the recipient of the Presidential Medal of Freedom) Eric Hoffer!

For nearly three decades there have been numerous other posthumously published books offered for public consumption having to do with Bruce Lee's fighting methods. It is in no way coincidental that the publisher of most of these books also publishes the leading martial arts magazine,

Black Belt.

Does anyone believe that it is mere coincidence that until just recently Bruce Lee has dominated practically every issue of Black Belt magazine since his death in July 1973? Years ago grand national champion Gracie Cassallas wrote a letter of protest to the editor saying "Enough already!" But the issue of Bruce Lee monopolizing nearly three decades of Black Belt, and thus helping to create the legend of Bruce Lee, isn't the real tragedy. What is pitiful is that Black Belt magazine, traditionally for over forty years being the voice (and often the watchdog) of the martial arts community at large, was arguably the vehicle through which years of investigative and factual reporting into the life and death of Bruce Lee should have been voiced.

In 1992 the executive editor of Black Belt was made aware of the general content of this book. following a common practice, several sample chapters were sent to the Black Belt (as well as several other magazines) for their consideration as feature stories, a book review, and future advertising. Although one of the magazine's assistant editors expressed a sincere interest in the material, a letter of response was sent to the author, stating "You supplied us with some very interesting material, and we would LOVE to use some of it. However, my superiors have close ties to Linda Lee and will not allow us to." Unfortunately, as the world learned from the fiasco of the O.J. Simpson trial, personal financial agendas, biased media, hero imagery, and a search for the truth are by definition too often in direct conflict.

Over the years Adrian Marshall has instituted numerous lawsuits against those he believed were guilty of a wide range of transgressions. Among the list of defendants:

Aquarius Films, Eternal Films of Hong Kong, Herman Cohen Productions, Cinema Shares of New York, Spectacular Films of Hong Kong, films of America, Allied Artists, Hallmark, Esquire, and Winthrop. In addition, not long after Bruce's death, Marshall represented Linda Lee in a landmark $10,000,000 lawsuit against Allied Artists, naming as co-plaintiffs Betty Ting-pei, Madame Lo Wei, and Raymond Chow, of all people, who, individually and collectively, Marshall charged had been "exposed to contempt and ridicule and caused great mental and emotional anguish and distress, embarrassment and humiliation." Within a short time, Betty Ting and Madame Lo Wei had sense enough to request that their names be dropped from what was inevitably viewed as a frivolous and meritless action.

Immediately after Bruce Lee's death, and during the years that Bruce's estate was being probated, Linda and Adrian traveled extensively together to Hawaii, New England, Europe, and the Orient. As the estate's bank accounts grew, Linda and Adrian purchased property and entered into business partnerships together, with Linda often putting up Adrian's share of the investment capital. Apart from the substantial legal fees Marshall was paid as the attorney for Bruce's estate, almost from the day Bruce Lee died, Marshall has owned, in perpetuity, 25 percent of all revenue generated through the merchandising of Bruce Lee, this in addition to a handsome annual retainer fee. Having ended his law partnership with Bryant Burton within a short time after Bruce died, Marshall has for the past three decades worked out of his home in Long Beach, his sole client being that of Linda Lee.

Regarding the final accounting of the Bruce Lee

Estate, prior to appearing in a Los Angeles probate court in September 1979, Marshall became concerned that he had not kept sufficient records to substantiate his years of legal fees and, as a result, instructed Linda to petition the court to waive a detailed accounting.

Unamused, the executives at Peat, Marwick, Mitchell, and Company promptly wrote to Marshall, advising him that they would be forced to make certain disclaimers to the court in "matters of this kind," specifically that the cash accounts did not purport to present the financial position of the estate because accounts receivable and accounts payable had been omitted, that the accounts had not been prepared in accordance with generally accepted accounting principles, that certain footnotes necessary for proper disclosure had been omitted, and that no audit steps were taken in the course of preparing the transcription, not even the verification of bank account cash balances.

On October 4, 1979 Petitioner Linda Lee, acting as the Executrix of the Estate of Bruce Lee, presented the following document (Exhibit 1) to the court for its approval: "For my information and use a detailed accounting (of my husband's estate) has been prepared by the international accounting firm of Peat, Marwick, Mitchell & Co. for the period November 1, 1976 to September 17, 1979. I have examined the accounting. However, a summary accounting only is being presented to the Court, and I hereby waive the presentation of a detailed accounting to the probate court."

For the record, Adrian Marshall had previously traveled to Hong Kong in late January 1979 and terminated the services of Peat, Marwick, Mitchell & Company, as well as Johnson, Stokes and Masters, replacing both companies with the Hong Kong firm of Hampton, Winter and Glynn.

Following the Report of Administration, the court awarded both Linda and Adrian their requested, and quite substantial, extraordinary fees, after which Linda Lee received the entire proceeds of the Estate of Bruce Lee, which amounted in total to $2,448,559.47.

Late that afternoon, the following was entered into the public record: "It appearing that all acts of Linda Lee as Administrator were performed as required by law; it is ordered, adjudged and decreed; that Linda Lee as Administrator be discharged as such and sureties are hereby released from liability for all acts subsequent hereto. Dated December 27, 1979 and signed by Superior Court Judge Jack W. Swink." As the sun set on the western horizon, Bruce Lee was finally laid to rest for the second time.

As a significant footnote, the romance between Linda and Adrian continued for a few more years, ending finally in 1983. When asked in August 1988 how long her discreet relationship had gone on with Marshall, Linda replied, "about ten years."

CHAPTER 16

Game of Death

There is a scene in The Way of the Dragon in which Bruce and his leading lady Nora Miao are walking over a bridge. In the distance is a picturesque setting of lush gardens and pristine waterfalls. Nora pauses to admire the scenery, then explains how the gardens had been built by an ancient king for his queen. "Must have cost a lot of money," she sighs wistfully. "He must have really loved her. How do you like it?"

Bruce stares briefly at the gardens, then looks at Nora indignantly. "A big waste! All of this! In Hong Kong I would build on it, make money!" In essence, Bruce's words aptly describe the basic principle underlying the making of Game of Death: "Build on it and make money!"

To fully understand the afternoon of July 20, 1973, it is important to understand how Bruce Lee's last movie Game of Death, which was filmed posthumously, came into existence.

Following the completion of The Way of the Dragon and before the start-up of Enter the Dragon, recall that

Bruce, around October 1972, shot several fight sequences in Hong Kong with his foremost student Dan Inosanto, Laker basketball star Kareem Abdul-Jabbar, and hapkido master Ji Han Jai. This footage was shot on the spur of the moment and without a script.

When Enter the Dragon was given a green light in late November 1972, the fight footage Bruce had shot with Inosanto, Kareem Abdul-Jabbar, and Master Ji Han Jai was placed in cold storage at Golden Harvest. Technically the footage was owned jointly by Raymond Chow, who supplied the camera equipment and sets, and Bruce Lee, who supplied the talent.

Incontrovertibly, had Bruce not died, this footage would have never found its way onto the movie screen anywhere in the world. There are several reasons for this. Topping the list, Bruce did not look physically well. As a result of having temporarily discontinued his use of anabolic steroids, which he did not resume until December 1972 in preparation for Enter the Dragon in January 1973, Bruce had again shed nearly twenty pounds of muscle, and his face looked gaunt and pale. To many, the sight of Bruce wearing a washed-out yellow jumpsuit that hung on him like a wet dishrag was heartbreaking. It was hardly coincidental that Game of Death was the only film starring Bruce Lee in which he did not appear bare-chested. As to his performance, the spark that had previously ignited a dynamic explosion of energy was poignantly absent, and in the scenes with his protégé Dan Inosanto, the two men appeared evenly matched.

Unfortunately, however, in the wake of Bruce's death, someone or some group of people started brain storming the idea of marketing this fight footage of Bruce in combat with Inosanto, Kareem Abdul-Jabbar, and Master Ji Han Jai. Essentially, this became the skeletal footage upon which to "build on and make money!"

Collectively, once edited, the three fight sequences amounted to about fifteen minutes running time. In order to release a feature-length movie showcasing this footage, Raymond Chow needed another 100 minutes of film. After purchasing the rights to the footage from Linda Lee for US$200,000, Chow set out to find an actor to impersonate her deceased husband.

Following a massive advertising campaign throughout which there was absolutely no mention that the producers were in search of a Bruce Lee double, auditions were held at Universal Studios in what was best described as a mad circus. After several exhausting days, a panel of judges, which include Linda Lee, singled out a young Chinese man from over a thousand contestants of all sizes, shapes and nationalities. While Bruce's double got busy working on his Bruce Lee impersonation, Raymond Chow addressed his second problem, that of coming up with a script.

Screenwriter Jan Spears was hired to develop a story that would showcase the fifteen minutes of fight footage Bruce had previously filmed in Hong Kong. The task was monumental, and Spears literally constructed the script form scratch. This is evident from the final screen credits of Game of Death, in which Spears is given a sole writing credit, with no reference given to "story by" or "adapted from." Had there been an earlier draft of Game of Death, or even a treatment (which some people would have us believe), Spears would not have received a sole writing credit.

Furthermore, had an original script or treatment penned by Bruce Lee ever existed, it surely would have been auctioned along with Bruce's other personal possessions in either of the two public auctions arranged by Linda.

Unquestionably the general storyline of Game of Death is utterly bizarre. The leading man (our Bruce Lee impersonator) plays a Hong Kong film star known the world over as the "King of Kung Fu." In the opening scenes, Lee is being muscled by organized crime figures (triads), who are demanding that he sign a management contract. Starting to sound familiar? Lee refuses and soon threatens to go to the police and expose the extortion ring. Following several attempts on Bruce's life (the last of which has Lee being shot in the face while filming a movie, the bullet being shot from a prop gun that was supposed to be loaded with blanks), our hero eventually lands in the witness protection program, complete with a fake funeral. Of course, there's an inevitable women-in-danger crisis (flagrantly structured to resemble Lee's real life relationship with Betty Ting-pei), and Lee's agent (coincidentally with the last name of Marshall) who, in the closing scenes, is warned by one of the triads: "You can learn a lot in a job like yours. But knowledge can become a terrible burden."

Throughout the picture, the Bruce Lee double hides (and fights!) behind designer sunglasses, which he also wears indoors and at night, and later, owing to having been shot in the face, plays entire scenes with his head wrapped in bandages, giving him the ludicrous appearance of a battling Egyptian mummy. This to be followed by the dreadful full beard and mustache disguise, and later the unimaginative old man masquerade, all of which is interspersed with actual

Chapter 17

July 20, 1973 Re-visited

"When the doctors left Bruce's side, I stayed with him to assure myself that there really was nothing I could do. It was at this point, when his life force was barely extinguished, that I felt an incredible strength surge through my body and spirit. The determination and courage of Bruce himself passed to me."

• Linda Lee

When I first heard the general explanation of what had occurred on the day Bruce Lee died in Hong Kong, it made me uncomfortable. Knowing what I know today, I am considerably more uncomfortable. What follows is surely not entirely correct. It is, however, a more logical interpretation of the available information. At the very least, it corrects much of the absurdity of the basic story (Chapters 7 & 9) as it has been told for the past twenty-nine years.

To better understand the afternoon of July 20, 1973, we need to first examine where Bruce was in terms of his film career at that time.

Although Enter the Dragon had not yet been released, it was generally agreed that Bruce Lee was on the verge of international stardom and that he was returning to the United States. If this was true, then why all this discussion about Raymond Chow, Betty Ting, and Bruce Lee spending so much time rewriting the script to Game of Death? Clearly, Bruce had finally accomplished his Chief Aim in Life. Hollywood was banging on his door. Apart from the fact that there wasn't even a script to rewrite, even if there had been a script to Game of Death, it makes no sense that Bruce would have been in any rush to get the film produced, for on the day Bruce died he didn't need Raymond Chow, or Golden Harvest, or Concord, or Game of Death. All he had to do was call Ted Ashley at Warner Brothers and tell him he wanted the top three available writers in Hollywood placed at his disposal, along with a plate of oyster beef and hot tea served at his private bungalow at the Beverly Hills Hotel, or anywhere else for that matter, and he would have gotten all of it. And what's more, he knew it because he'd hung out with Steve McQueen and James Coburn and Stirling Silliphant and so he knew all about Tinseltown's million-dollar packaging agents and business managers and entertainment lawyers, and you can bet all of them were eagerly calling Bruce Lee.

This, however, is not the picture that's been painted by Raymond Chow, Betty Ting, and Linda Lee for the past twenty-nine years. On July 20, 1973 Bruce is a hurried man. Raymond Chow arrives at Lee's house, and the men sit for hours pouring over final rewrites. Amazing as it sounds, Raymond has suddenly become Bruce's writing partner.

The clock is ticking. The ink is still wet on the pages. As typhoon Dorothy begins to unleash its initial fury, they rush over to the apartment of Betty Ting-pei, a C-rated actress, to offer her a part in Bruce's next film. God willing, she will accept in time for the three of them to then drive to the Miramar Hotel to wine and dine George Lazenby, in the hope that he, too, will accept a part. Two weeks earlier Bruce had turned down a role to star with Elvis Presley, yet he's rushing through the day in the hope of starring with B-rated actor Lazenby. Ten weeks earlier Bruce had collapsed at Golden Harvest and had been rushed to Baptist Hospital on the verge of death. And now, rather than recuperating, he's feverishly racing all over town with a Hong Kong producer, a C-rated Taiwanese actress, and George Lazenby, with barely enough time to partake in two soft drinks throughout the entire day, only to lie down that evening with a splitting headache. It's an utterly absurd scenario. Bruce may have had little choice but to tolerate this kind of day six months earlier, but he obviously had no reason to do so on July 20, 1973. So what's wrong with the basic story?

The first problem has to do with the general atmosphere surrounding Raymond Chow's early afternoon appearance at Cumberland Road. Clearly he wasn't there to work with Bruce rewriting Game of Death. So why the visit? There are two reasonable possibilities.

The first has to do with Bruce's ongoing battle with an assortment of potentially volatile drugs. We know that his last episode of raging occurred only ten days earlier at Golden Harvest Studios when he threatened to kill director Lo Wei. Besides Bruce's tormenting physiological nightmare, he was well known for his short fuse and explosive temper. All things considered, it is very conceivable that for any one of a long list of reasons Bruce had again gone on a rampage, resulting in Linda summoning Raymond Chow.

Alternatively, and more likely, it is very conceivable that Raymond Chow, fearful that he was losing his million-dollar star and in a state of desperation, drove to Cumberland Road to plead with Bruce to stay in business. Besides Bruce having stated both publicly and privately that he was returning to the U.S. to work for the majors in Hollywood, the two men had for months been arguing over the business end of The Way of the Dragon.

To begin with, it was well known that Bruce was upset over Raymond's having made distribution deals without first discussing it with him. Second and far worse was the problem that Concord had reported to the press that the film was a smash hit, and yet the company's cash revenues didn't equate with its reported box-office receipts. If there is any substance to the notion of triad involvement in The Way of the Dragon, the triad kingpins would have wanted an explanation of what surely would have appeared to be two sets of books. Coincidentally, it was around this time that Bruce's brother Peter began making public statements about Bruce growing suspicious that Raymond had not been giving him a fair box-office accounting of The Way of the Dragon. In any event, one could surmise that with Bruce's plans to return to the United States, any problem concerning the triads, if there indeed was one, was being dumped solely in Raymond's lap.

For the past twenty-nine years many people have questioned why Cumberland Road had suddenly and curiously turned into a ghost town on July 20, 1973. Normally the Lee house was akin to Grand Central Station, what with being home to two large families and with a backyard often overrun with children. So the obvious question is, where was everyone? Linda claims to have gone to lunch with Rebu Hui, the wife of pop singer Sam Hui. Besides Linda, where was Wu Ngan? And where was Ngan's wife? Also gone? Who was watching all the children? Gone, too? The point is, where were all these people who could have verified the events of that afternoon? Their collective absence just sounds all too convenient.

As to the real reason behind Raymond Chow's appearance at Cumberland Road that day, the answer is probably known only to Raymond Chow, Linda Lee, Rebu Hui, Betty Ting, and probably Wu Ngan. All things considered, what seems certain is that something went on that day at Cumberland Road that no one wants to talk about. And whatever it is, it would appear that, among other things, thirty years ago it made Lee's house servant Wu Ngan a very rich man.

No matter how their initial meeting turned out, at approximately four o'clock Raymond and Bruce left Bruce's home and drove to Betty Ting's apartment.

Curiously, at the inquest the issue of the time was raised more than once. The Crown Counsel, Joe Duffy, questioned Raymond Chow: "Would there be any truth to suggestions that you arrived at Miss Ting-pei's flat at three o'clock in the afternoon with Mr. Lee, and not four or five p.m.?" Raymond Chow heatedly denied this and went on to explain that such could not have been possible because they had been studying a new script. Aside from the fact that Chow's answer wasn't true, it was a totally meaningless response.

As to why Bruce and Raymond went to Betty's, there are again several possible answers. First, Raymond may have simply driven Bruce to Betty's because Bruce could not park his flashy Mercedes in front of Betty's apartment due to the ongoing publicity surrounding their affair. Secondly, in the event that Bruce had gone on another rampage, Raymond may have sought Betty's help in calming him down. And third, if motivated by business, Raymond may have driven Bruce to Betty's in the hope that she could have been helpful in convincing Bruce to remain in Hong Kong. But the important point is that whatever their reason for going to Betty's, Bruce and Raymond did not drive to her apartment to work with her on Game of Death or to offer her a part in any movie. Betty wasn't a writer. She was Bruce's lover. And if he wanted her to co-star in his next picture, then she would co-star in his next picture. Period.

Upon their arrival at Betty's, Raymond accompanied Bruce inside for a short time, apparently just long enough to finish a soft drink, and then left, after reiterating that he hoped Bruce and Betty would be able to join him and Lazenby later for dinner. Bruce and Betty were now alone. What happened next was what had been happening for months. Bruce got high on marijuana, and perhaps other drugs, and ended up with Betty in her bedroom where they may or may not have made love. Several hours elapsed, and they probably either passed out or fell asleep, most likely having unplugged the phone. At the inquest, Betty's sworn testimony was that from the time she first gave Bruce the single tablet of Equagesic until approximately four hours later when she discovered him in a coma she had remained alone in the living room watching television. Yes, that was her testimony.

Around 7:30 that evening Betty was either awakened by Bruce convulsing or she awoke on her own to discover Bruce had lapsed into what she believed was a coma. She called Raymond at the Miramar Hotel where he was having dinner with Lazenby.

It is at this point that Raymond and Betty have a fair chance of saving Bruce's life. Clearly there can be little doubt that Bruce is undergoing the same problem he had encountered on May 10. Baptist Hospital is only blocks away. Either Betty or Raymond can call an ambulance and have Bruce transported to Baptist where doctors, acutely familiar with Bruce's previous collapse, will instantly know to administer Mannitol, thus relieving the increasing cerebral-spinal fluid pressure in Bruce's brain. But neither Betty nor Raymond does that. Instead, Raymond spends twenty minutes driving over to Betty's apartment through a raging storm.

Upon his arrival, Betty again informs Raymond that she cannot awaken Bruce, even by slapping his face. Although Raymond thinks Bruce looks normal, he can't awaken him either. Does he call an ambulance, knowing what happened to Bruce on May 10? No. What does he do? He slaps Bruce around and shakes him violently for ten minutes! Failing to awaken Bruce, does he then call an ambulance? No. He calls Betty's personal physician, Dr. Chu Pho-hwye. Chu's line is busy, but Raymond keeps trying and finally gets through. As unbelievable as it sounds, on May 10 at Golden Harvest Studios, Chow found himself in practically this same predicament. There was the ticking clock pitted against Bruce in a fight for his life, and Raymond Chow calling over to Baptist asking to talk with a physician.

Another twenty minutes elapse while Dr. Chu drives over to Betty's. Does Chu call an ambulance? No. What does he do? He slaps Bruce around for ten minutes and at some point begins to have difficulty finding a pulse!

Finally Chu decides to have Bruce transported to a hospital. Baptist Hospital is just a few short blocks away. Does Dr. Chu order Bruce rushed to Baptist? No. He has the ambulance driver transport him clear across town to Queen Elizabeth Hospital where Bruce is pronounced dead on arrival.

As a footnote to this Gothic horror story, when Brian Tisdall, who was Linda Lee's Hong Kong attorney and represented her at the inquest, asked Dr. Chu why he had not sent Bruce to Baptist Hospital instead of Queen Elizabeth, Chu testified: "Bruce Lee deeply comatose, pulse not acceptable, no respiration, pupils not fully dilated. When he did not show any sings of improvement, it did not occur to me that time was of great importance."

One can hardly believe such an outrageous statement was offered in defense of what would appear at face value to be an act of gross and unconscionable malpractice. So there is something wrong here.

The problem is that Dr. Chu's testimony left out one vital fact, if for no other reason than no one ever asked. Recall that Raymond Chow testified that upon his arrival at Betty's it appeared to him that Bruce looked perfectly normal. When Bruce arrived at Queen Elizabeth Hospital, where he was pronounced dead on arrival, his face was swollen like a watermelon. Now if Raymond Chow is telling the truth, then one has to question when exactly did Bruce's face become swollen? If Bruce looked normal to Raymond prior to being taken from Betty's in an ambulance, and he was dead on arrival at Queen Elizabeth Hospital, then the grotesque swelling of Bruce's face could have only occurred during the twenty-minute ambulance ride to the hospital. In order for this to have occurred, Bruce's heart would have had to be beating. This, however, did not occur because according to Dr. Chu's testimony Bruce did not have a pulse.

That's a pretty serious matter, isn't it? Not having a pulse? Add to that the fact that Bruce wasn't breathing and that his pupils weren't dilating and one has to question why Dr. Chu didn't immediately start pounding on Bruce's chest while either Raymond or Betty breathed air into his lungs? The answer is obvious. The important testimony that Dr. Chu could have given had someone asked was that when Dr. Chu arrived at Betty's, Bruce Lee was already dead and had been for some time.

How did Bruce Lee really die? This is the focus of the next two chapters.

CHAPTER 18

The Devil's Due

"It's like I'm in jail! I am like the monkey in the zoo!"

• Bruce Lee

Near the end of his life, Bruce privately said to Linda, "I don't know how much longer I can keep this up." What exactly was Bruce talking about? Was he referring to his rigorous training schedules or his demanding movie career? Perhaps the complexities of corporate business? OR maybe he was talking about the pitfalls of instant fame and fortune? The fact is Bruce wasn't talking about any of this. The problem confronting Bruce Lee near the end of his life was that his runaway drug use had finally turned his world into a nightmare of spinning plates.

Because of his childhood cryptorchidism and his obsessive personality, Bruce Lee was unquestionably a poor candidate for anabolic steroids. Antithetically, although it seems unlikely that his initial interest in taking male hormone had to do with increasing his sex drive, it is understandable how Bruce would have been attracted to steroids from a martial artist's point of view. Besides developing and building muscle mass, steroids dramatically increased Bruce's speed and power. In the late 1960s these miracle drugs succeeded in helping him rise to the upper echelon of the martial arts world. As he entered his movie career in the early 1970s, anabolic steroids coupled with diuretics were greatly responsible for the streamlined muscular body well known to movie-goers.

Inevitably, however, the adverse side effects appeared. Trying to ward off his increasing anxiety, insomnia, and terrifying outbursts of rage, Bruce stepped up his use of prescription drugs, primarily CNS depressants and anti-anxiety medications, and soon began abusing marijuana and alcohol.

It would prove to be a race against time. His Chief Aim in Life was on the horizon. Ten million dollars and his name in lights, and then he would live a life of peace and harmony. If only he could keep this up for another month. Everyone told him he was close to succeeding. Enter the Dragon was assured to make him a star. It didn't matter. Time was too quickly running out. Bruce had to break the cycle. He had to stop taking anabolic steroids. Having confided in his wife that he just couldn't keep going any longer, he finally told Raymond Chow that he has made his last martial arts movie.

Within a few weeks of quitting steroids, Bruce's muscles began to atrophy, more so than ever before. The problem, well known to other users, was that in taking anabolic steroids, his body's natural ability to produce testosterone had been severely diminished. As a result, at least figuratively speaking, Bruce's cryptorchidism returned. Only now, instead of manufacturing a substandard level of testosterone, his body produced almost none. Soon Bruce's weight dropped below 120 pounds. His beard growth diminished and his hands became soft and silken.

As horrifying as it was, the only way to reverse the demasculating process and recapture his identity he would sooner be dead than without was to again resume taking steroids. To do so, however, meant almost certain risk of serious liver and heart damage, and, even worse, the return of roid raging. In sharp contrast, to remain steroid-free meant more than just the severe muscle deterioration and energy loss. It would mean the end to the invincible King of Kung Fu.

Tragically, the demons Bruce confronted as a result of his use of steroids paled in comparison to the physiological horrors unleashed by his physical and psychological addiction to cortisone.

Recall that immediately following the death of Bruce Lee, several brown paper bags containing crudely made bombs began to appear in and around Hong Kong. the message written on several of the bags was peculiar. It read: "Betty knows the cause of Bruce Lee's death." Note that the message did not say that Betty knows who had killed Bruce Lee, but rather that she knew the cause of his death. It was a provocative message, whose meaning may be related to the following portion of Dr. Harold Karpman's sworn deposition on July 24, 1974, which he gave in Los Angeles to one of Linda's attorneys, John Healey, around the time of the Lloyds/AIA insurance matter:

Q: What other physicians to your knowledge have treated Mr. Lee?
A: To my knowledge, Dr. Reisbord saw him here. I know that I had his pathological report reviewed by Dr. Ronald Okun, who is a toxicologist at the University. But he never saw Mr. Lee. And then there was a physician in Hong Kong whose name was—an English physician, I think. I heard a name cursorily, but I can't remember the name.
Q: Dr. Langford?
A: It could be. That's all I know. In this country only myself and Dr. Reisbord saw him at that time.
Q: Do you know of a Dr. Tanney?
A: Herb Tanney?
Q: Right.
A: Yes. I know Herb Tanney.
Q: Do you know that Dr. Tanney had been treating him [Lee] in the past?
A: No, I didn't know that. When was that? I mean, prior to the time he [Lee] went to Hong Kong?
Q: Yes. This would have been '70, '71.
A: No, I didn't know that. I really didn't know that at all.

Why would John Healey be interested in questioning Karpman about Dr. Tanney's professional relationship to Bruce Lee three years earlier, particularly if one presumes that Bruce hadn't seen Tanney since moving to Hong Kong in October 1971? The answer is to be found in the second portion of Dr. Karpman's deposition:
Q: He [Lee] didn't mention anything about sustaining a back injury and being on cortisone for a great period of time?

A: No.
Q: Again, had you know that, would that in any way—
A: No, cortisone is not going to influence this in any way.
Q: I heard it might make him more conducive to seizures.
A: If you take massive amounts by injection. Most people take it by injection. It's very unlikely that you could get a sufficient amount of cortisone into the system to produce any metabolic response if you take it orally.

What is tragic about the above exchange is that throughout his deposition, Karpman does not ask, nor is he told, about how often and how much cortisone Bruce was receiving and whether it was by injection or orally. In all likelihood the reason Karpman was somewhat indifferent about this issue was that at the time of the deposition the consensus of the medical profession was that the use of cortisone was a safe and benign practice.

Prior to Bruce's departure to Hong Kong in October 1971 we know that he received a full year of cortisone injections from Dr. Herbert Tanney. The details of his continued use of cortisone over the next two years, however, are difficult to piece together, especially regarding how Bruce was being supplied the drug and in what amounts. Nevertheless, based on his medical history and the observations of those around him in the final months of his life, there is no doubt that Bruce was in a constant uphill battle with adrenal insufficiency as a direct result of his long-standing use of cortisone.

Initially Bruce Lee was injected with cortisone to reduce musculoskeletal inflammation in areas of his back, knees, and hands. Within a short time, however, he began to rely on the drug to combat a smattering of physical ailments, both real and imagined, and began to experience mood elevations and an increase in sex drive. Remember that this was nearly three decades ago. Today Bruce's prolonged use of cortisone, and more importantly his withdrawal from this powerful drug, would be closely monitored. Owing to years of extensive scientific research, today physicians approach the clinical use of cortisone with extreme caution.

The central problem confronting Bruce Lee as a result of his extended use of cortisone was that the drug had caused his adrenal glands to atrophy and, as a result, his body's natural ability to produce hydrocortisone had been dramatically decreased. One major function of this steroid is to support circulation in cases of stress. When a normal person develops an illness or sustains an injury, the adrenal glands "kick out" a "booster dose" of hydrocortisone to help maintain capillary tone and support blood pressure. If a patient with adrenal atrophy sustains an injury or develops an illness, there is no hydrocortisone to be kicked out and the capillary system can collapse and death ensues. A second product of the adrenal glands is cortisol, which is vital to protein and carbohydrate metabolism. Lacking sufficient amounts of cortisol, Bruce's body was unable to properly metabolize food.

The most prominent symptom noted in patients suffering from chronic adrenal insufficiency is a general wasting away of the body. In addition to a loss of appetite and accompanying weight loss, the patient frequently battles dehydration. Within a few months, the individual experiences muscle weakness and fatigue (tragically Bruce may have attributed this to his discontinuance of anabolic steroids). Due to falling blood pressure the person at times feels faint and dizzy and mental confusion, including bouts of amnesia, is often noted. Besides stomach pain, nausea and vomiting are also frequently noted. But most important of all is the telltale sign common to the great majority of patients—the brownish skin (that looks suntanned) with white patches coupled with the darkening of freckles on the face and neck. All of the above symptoms were periodically noted in Bruce Lee during the last six months of his life.

Is it possible that the King of Kung Fu died of the unchecked, fatal complications of adrenal crisis? If he did, it would explain the mysterious BUN laboratory test result that surfaced at Baptist Hospital following Bruce's collapse on May 10, for it is a fact that with adrenal insufficiency the body's level of blood urea nitrogen literally soars.

Although it has been previously established that the symptoms noted in Bruce when he collapsed at Golden Harvest on May 10 and his death ten weeks later on July 20 were remarkably similar, were these same symptoms common to someone suffering the throes of acute adrenal crisis? The answer is a qualified yes. By now acutely familiar with the adverse side effects of cortisone, Bruce would have instantly recognized the initial symptoms of adrenal insufficiency. A rising intracranial pressure would have triggered a headache, and he would have felt nauseous and fatigued. Had he not increased his body's level of cortisone, he inevitably would have lapsed into adrenal crisis, which is a life-threatening medical emergency of the highest magnitude. Had Bruce administered the correct amount of cortisone, however, his symptoms would have rapidly subsided.

Over time and considering the odds, Bruce would

have been better off playing Russian roulette, for it is today well known to medical professionals that attempting to self-regulate one's own level of cortisone without the aid of laboratory tests and without consulting a physician is an extremely dangerous practice. To say the least, it's a delicate recipe. Take too little and the result is a continuing uphill battle against adrenal insufficiency. Take too much over too short a period and the body rehydrates so speedily that vomiting and high fever are soon followed by convulsions, cerebral edema and coma.

Perhaps this is what occurred to Bruce Lee on the afternoon of July 20, 1973. Deprived of sufficient adrenal hormones and feeling the side effects of an impending adrenal crisis, Bruce self-administered too much cortisone while he was at Cumberland Road. A short while later, upon his arrival at Betty's apartment, he drank several cold sodas in response to his rising temperature. Almost immediately his body's water balance went haywire and his tissues began retaining fluids at an alarming rate while his kidneys began to shut down. Headache set in, and Betty gave him Equagesic in an effort to suppress the pain and lower his fever. It didn't help. Bruce lied down in Betty's bedroom where his body continued to overhydrate. Within a short time the life-threatening medical emergency ran its unchecked course as Bruce experienced convulsions, cerebral edema and fatal coma. Using this same case scenario, the reason that Bruce Lee would have survived the identical life-threatening emergency on May 10 at Golden Harvest was simply because the doctors at Baptist Hospital had administered Mannitol, thus relieving the rapid rehydration process that had been caused by a similar cortisone overdose.

Ironically, Bruce would have reached the same life-threatening emergency had he not administered any cortisone at all. In the absence of sufficient hydrocortisone, his body's circulatory system, and thus his capillary tone, would have gradually begun to collapse, resulting in fluids being retained in his tissues. Within a short time his kidneys would have shut down, leading to convulsions and brain edema. In the end, coma and death. As to the May 10 incident, under the above scenario Bruce would have miraculously recovered once he had arrived at Baptist Hospital because, in addition to Mannitol, doctors would have eventually detected a falling blood pressure and immediately administered an injection of hydrocortisone. This is a routine procedure done in any emergency room crisis when an unexplained sudden drop in blood pressure is noted. Having been injected with hydrocortisone, Bruce's symptoms would have gradually subsided and he would have returned to normal.

Although the overall clinical picture of adrenal-cortical insufficiency described above has a profound and unsettling resemblance to the physical description of Bruce Lee in the final months of his life, there is still one major hurdle to get over. And that is simply this. Recall that just weeks following Bruce's collapse on May 10, he and Linda traveled to Los Angeles where Bruce underwent a thorough medical examination, including a battery of sophisticated tests. At its conclusion, aside form a minor convulsive disorder, the doctors could find nothing the matter with him. Why was this? One answer could be simply that between the time of Lee's May 10 collapse at Golden Harvest and his arrival in Los Angeles several weeks later, his body's level of corticosteroid had been restored.

Russian roulette is a dangerous game, but there are

survivors who live to spin the barrel again. To present day medical doctors it is not uncommon that many patients with some adrenal function but limited reserves appear perfectly healthy until something precipitates the next adrenal crisis. This condition when associated with steroid use is particularly treacherous, as the "common finding" in Addison's disease (primary adrenal failure) of a low serum sodium is not present when the suppression is due to exogenous (self-administered) steroids. In addition, one must not lose sight of the time frame. This was the early 1970s when the horrors of cortisone abuse were practically unknown to the medical profession. To that end, even had Bruce mentioned his use of cortisone, it is conceivable that his physicians may not have placed much value on it. And lastly, to have properly diagnosed Bruce's problem at that time, it would have been necessary for the doctors to have ordered an extensive battery of adrenal hormone and adrenal gland function tests. Had Bruce's level of cortisone been within normal limits, such additional tests would not have been routinely ordered, particularly in the early 1970s.

In conclusion, did Bruce's life end as a direct result of adrenal crisis associated with brain edema? Based on the material submitted to them, the medical professionals with whom I consulted unanimously concluded that it is a good possibility. They were quick to point out, however, a single option. If Bruce Lee did not die of adrenal crisis, there remains only one reasonable, and deadly, alternative explanation...

Chapter 19

Foul Play

As soon as the Hong Kong police learned of the death of Bruce Lee, the first thing they did was hit the streets in search of Bruce's drug connections. They knew something the rest of us hadn't taken seriously. They knew that there were people out there that wanted Bruce Lee dead.

Like everyone else, the police were quite familiar with Bruce's mistress Betty Ting. Weeks earlier she had tried to kill herself because Bruce had wanted out of the affair. She had links to both organized crime and drugs.

The police also knew that the triads had been hounding Bruce for months. Millions of dollars were on the line. And what about all those foreign producers who were standing in bread line because the King of Kung Fu had totally wiped out their distribution market? There seemed to be suspects popping up on every corner. The lead detective opened a file and labeled it a probable homicide. He never called Wyeth Laboratories to ask about the side effects of Equagesic. He would rather talk to that elusive butler Bruce

Lee had given his worldly possessions to. Then there was this business about a falling out with Raymond Chow. Without Bruce Lee, Golden Harvest Studios would be making rice commercials.

By day two of the investigation the detectives were pounding on doors all over Hong Kong. Who were these martial arts elders Bruce Lee had offended? And where was this triad that Lee had beaten into submission on the set of Enter the Dragon? Was it true that Bruce had paid off the guy's family? And why was Linda Lee acting so scared? The autopsy report wasn't even in yet and she was already announcing to the world that she didn't hold anyone or any group responsible for her husband's death. The police thought it a little premature. And who was this lawyer from California feverishly racing around Hong Kong looking for bank accounts? Yes, Hollywood didn't have anything over Hong Kong. This was a real rags-to-riches story that had everything but a plane crash.

The police weren't the only ones who were treating this as a homicide. Weeks earlier the doctors over at Baptist Hospital took one look at Bruce and presumed he'd been poisoned. They were simply following procedure, and it's the same throughout the world. Walk into any hospital emergency room and tell the attending physician that there is a patient on route who is exhibiting symptoms of cerebral edema and kidney failure, and immediately that physician will open a line to the Poison Control Center. The reason he will do this is because cerebral edema combined with acute renal failure is a common sign of poisoning.

From a clinical standpoint, poisoning is always considered in the diagnosis of any unexplained signs or symp toms. When Dr. Langford examined Bruce Lee at Baptist Hospital on May 10, he immediately ordered intravenous injections of Mannitol. The reason that Langford's choice of drug is noteworthy is that Mannitol is rarely used solely for the treatment of cerebral edema. Rather, it is an osmotic diuretic used primarily in barbiturate overdoses and to flush out the system of a potentially lethal excess of sodium, which many poisons can cause to collect in the victim's kidneys. It is this excess sodium buildup that produces the cerebral edema and convulsions, and it is for this reason that Langford administered Mannitol to Bruce Lee, specifically because Bruce was showing signs that he had been poisoned.

This would explain the mysterious blood urea nitrogen (BUN) test. It wasn't a typographical error as Dr. Harold Karpman had initially suspected. Although a reading of 92 (mg/ml) is extremely high, it is consistent with a patient whose kidneys had gone into failure as a result of being poisoned.

Poisoning Bruce Lee at this time in his life would not have been that easy. According to Linda, during her husband's final months, he had stopped eating solid food and was existing miserably on carrot and apple juice. If this was true, then the only way to have poisoned Bruce was to lace the one thing everyone knew he was eating—his marijuana.

The question now arises—where did Bruce Lee keep all this marijuana? This was not an insignificant amount, but a sizeable stash that was being replenished on a frequent basis. Of course, the most central problem was that Bruce was potentially a multimillion-dollar show business property. Unquestionably, his drug use had to be of dire concern to many individuals, especially in that his drug of choice was marijuana. Throughout the Orient in the early 1970s marijuana was tantamount to being found with heroin in the United States. Witness Beatles star Paul McCartney who nearly landed in prison after being discovered in Japan with a small amount of grass. No, there was too much money at stake here. Literally millions. Somebody else had to handle this marijuana. We know that Bobby Baker brought it into Hong Kong. But what happened to it after that? Perhaps it was locked in Bruce's 500-pound floor safe at Cumberland? Risky. What about Golden Harvest Studios? There was a guardhouse at the main entrance. Of course this hadn't stopped the police form barging into the place over the Lo Wei incident. Golden Harvest had a cold storage vault. How about in there? Or maybe it was kept at Betty Ting's apartment? What about Wu Ngan? Maybe Lee's faithful manservant was the entrusted one. Yes. Who kept watch over Bruce Lee's marijuana stash? Who was the keeper of the keys? There was motive all around Bruce. Access equates to opportunity. It is a vital piece of the puzzle.

Motive. Opportunity. Method. Poison. When Bruce Lee collapsed to the floor at Golden Harvest and suddenly began convulsing and vomiting and gasping in a fight for his life, that one word—poison—just seems to hang in the air. Nothing else but a heart attack or stroke or a bullet acts this quickly to extinguish a life. That is the one element of this entire scenario that keeps lighting up like one of Hong Kong's millions of neon lights. It is like a candle. One moment it's lit, and the next it's extinguished. One moment Bruce was in a desperate fight for his life, and an hour later, after the Mannitol had flushed his system, he miraculously returned to normal and walked out of the emergency room.

Poison.

What about Lee's autopsy? Did Dr. Lam look for poison? He did. Superficially. Worldwide there are 9,000,000 natural and synthetic chemicals deemed to be poisonous. Of these, 3,000 cause more than 95 percent of all the accidental and deliberate poisonings reported each year.

Generally speaking, the common procedure done at most autopsies is to conduct a random search for poison by testing for assorted trace metals. This is done because the majority of poisons contain at least one of several metals in their chemical makeup. Although in his testimony Dr. Lam was careful to avoid the word poison, clearly he was looking for poison when he tested for mercury and lead, which are two of the main trace metals common to many poisonous substances. Two trace elements Dr. Lam did not test for were fluoride and phosphorus. Both are found in poisons knows to cause convulsions, cerebral edema, and renal failure in their victims. Both fluoride and phosphorus are commonly found in rat poison and other common household pesticides.

Unfortunately, the fact is that if Bruce Lee died of poisoning, it was a premeditated act. More than likely a poison was used that would not be detected at autopsy. If one were to have need for such a unique poison, Hong Kong would surely be the place to go shopping. Kenpo Grandmaster Ed Parker must have known this when shortly after Bruce's death he was quoted as saying, "Many of us do not know the inner thinking and secrets of the Chinese herbalists. They have herbs for medicine and they have ones we've never heard of for poison. I believe it was foul play that killed Bruce Lee."

CHAPTER 20

Parting Thoughts

The writing of this book has been an extremely difficult and arduous endeavor. Like so many other authors and biographers who have walked this path before me, my perceptions of Bruce Lee have been forever changed. When I made my first discoveries, I must admit that I felt what I have since recognized as a misguided obligation to protect the "legend of Bruce Lee." I sweated out a great deal of writing time trying to find a way to justify the fact that the man I had once envisioned as a martial arts icon was, indeed, a human being fraught with human frailty and uncontrollable demons. Perhaps the toughest reality I have had to accept was the insight of Stirling Silliphant, who wisely pointed out that, in the end, the very thing that should have protected Bruce Lee—his martial art—failed him.

During the five years I have been writing and researching this book, I have been asked hundreds of questions by as many people. Yet there is one for which I still no answer. The question was asked by Amy Sanbo during my visit to her home on Vashon Island. I had been interviewing her for several hours when she suddenly asked, "Did you like Bruce?" I know now why I have so much trouble with that. It is because there are so many Bruce Lees. There's the

Chinese herb mixtures

one I first met in 1963 when I was a senior in high school. There is a different Bruce Lee who I knew in and around Hollywood. Then there is the husband Bruce Lee, as he was described to me by Linda. The best known is the commercialized King of Kung Fu Bruce Lee, which is an image often referred to as "Saint Bruce." The dilemma is that all these Bruce Lees are so vastly different from one another. Worse yet, I have mixed feelings about all of them. I can only imagine how painfully difficult this must have been for Bruce.

As I approached the first printing of this work in 1996, there was most assuredly trouble brewing on the horizon when I was threatened with massive civil litigation by three individuals should I proceed to publication. Raymond Chow, who refused numerous offers to talk with me about the content of this book, was represented by Beverly Hills attorney Michael Bergman. Moreover, Linda Lee Cadwell and Adrian Marshall, who also refused numerous offers to discuss the substance of this book, were jointly represented by Beverly Hills attorney Jerome Weinstein. For the record, since the first printing of Unsettled Matters, the statute of limitations ran out and none of these three individuals filed a lawsuit.

I was both saddened and disappointed that my former wife Linda chose not to offer anything constructive to the writing of this biography. It is true that when I began writing this book I fielded some criticism from a few individuals who felt that I displayed a degree of disloyalty to Linda by proceeding without her approval. It is perhaps a fair criticism. I would point out, however, that I was married to Linda for less than two years, while I have been a martial artists for over four decades. If I do have a loyalty in this matter it is to the martial arts community. I think collectively all of us deserve the truth and, frankly, I believe I was the only one who could have told this side of Bruce's life.

In my hear I truly believe that Bruce would have approved of this book. I say this because he never hid behind false pretenses. He was quite capable of standing on his own laurels. This was his stance in life. Good, bad, and indifferent. Bruce Lee was never afraid of the pure, unadulterated truth. In fact, he thrived on it, even demanded it of himself and everyone around him. The man had principles and he had tremendous courage and drive and they all conspired together in his final years to get him in trouble. That's the side of Bruce Lee I hope I have addressed. Why? What more can one ask of a fellow human being than to honestly share with us his life's greatest obstacles? To tell us about how he got in a jam and what he did to get out of it. As parents we don't do our children any favor by sitting around trying to convince them how great we are. They don't want to hear that. They want to know about how we get through life's problems. And it doesn't make Bruce a lesser person. Quite the contrary, it gives him a uniqueness because he was fortunate enough to live the life he led and to learn and to move forward with his own spiritual development. But it's of no value to any of us who remain behind if we aren't told the truth. This is why I wrote this book. I felt the time had come that we embrace Bruce Lee as a human being. All of us. We've become a society that thrives on truth. We're tired of being manipulated. There is great harm in fictionalizing Bruce Lee. I think it's damaging to the young people who walk into martial arts schools all over the world. We have great martial artists in this country who have to one degree or another stood in Bruce's shadow for the past twenty-nine years and all in the name of commercializing one man for the financial gain of a handful of individuals. This isn't to take anything away from Bruce. He will forever have his place in the martial arts. The man was a legendary shaker and a mover. Back then Bruce did some long overdue housecleaning. Thanks to Bruce they'll never again come a day where a man appoints himself a master and rises above the masses on some cloud of mystique without "proving himself," as Bruce used to say, and on a fairly regular basis. And we can all be proud of him for the tremendous contribution he's made to the art, but we have to put things in their proper perspective.

I wrote this book in the spirit of helping an old friend clean up the mess he left behind. This isn't solely about examining the possibility that someone or some group of people got away with a serious crime. Yes, that's a part of Bruce's past that's extremely important to me, but this book equally addresses the future. There are young people out there who can benefit greatly by knowing what happened to Bruce Lee. Despite how Bruce died, the pain and suffering that surrounded him and everyone around him in the final three years of his life would never have happened had he not become swept away by a current of obsessive living and mind sets.

Linda has often been quoted as saying that Bruce was a man who could do the things he said that he could. I wholeheartedly agree with her on this point. We can't change the past, but we can alter the future for the better if we stay as close to the truth as possible. As famed attorney

Chapter Twenty

Gerry Spence once wisely stated, we need to stick to the truth. For when we don't, half-truths eventually become whole lies.

Bibliography

Books

Barnhart, Edward R. Publisher. Physicians' Desk Reference. Oradell, New Jersey. Medical Economics Company, Inc. 1992

Berkow, Robert, M.D., Editor-in-Chief. The Merck Manual 15th Edition. Rahway, New Jersey. Merck Sharp & Dohme Research Laboratories. 1987.

Block, Alex Ben. The Legend of Bruce Lee. New York; Dell Publishing Co., Inc. 1974

Cleary, Thomas. The Japanese Art of War. Boston & London. Shambhala. 1992

Clouse, Robert. Bruce Lee: The Biography. Burbank, CA. Unique Publications, Inc. 1988

Gia-Fu Feng and Jane English. Tao Lao Tsu Te Ching. Vintage Books; Random House, New York. 1972.

Bibliography

Hill, Napoleon. Think & Grow Rich. Fawcett Books, New York. 1960.

Hui Fai, Editor. Bruce Lee: The Fighting Spirit. Hong Kong, Bruce Lee JKD Society. 1978.

Inosanto, Dan. Jeet Kune Do: The Art and Philosophy of Bruce Lee. Los Angeles, California. Know Now Publishing Company, 1976.

Lee, Linda. Bruce Lee: The Man Only I Knew. New York: Warner Paperbacks, 1975.

Lee, Linda and Tom Bleecker. The Bruce Lee Story. Burbank, CA. Ohara Publications, 1989.

Mushashi, Miyamoto. A Book of Five Rings. Woodstock, New York. The Overlook Press. 1982.

Nitobe, Inazo. Bushido: the Warrior's Code. Burbank, California. Ohara Publications, Inc. 1979.

Posner, Gerald L. Warlords of Crime, Chinese Secret Societies—the New Mafia. New York, McGraw Hill. 1988.

Robbins, Anthony. Unlimited Power. New York, Fawcett Columbine. 1986.

Speransky, A.D. The Revolutionary Pathology of A.D. Speransky. Frontiers of Medicine. 1986.

Thomas, Bruce. Bruce Lee: Fighting Spirit. Berkeley, California. Frog, Ltd. 1994.

Wong, Shun-leung. Reminiscence of Bruce Lee. Hong Kong, Bruce Lee JKD Society. Hui Fai, Editor. 1978.

Yip, Chun Master. 116 Wing Tsun Dummy Techniques. Leung Ting Publications, Hong Kong. 1981.

Magazines and government publications:

Asian Organized Crime. United States Senate Subcommittee on Investigations; 102 Congress. U.S. Government Printing Office, Washington. 1992

Asian Organized Crime: The New International Criminal. United States Senate Subcommittee on Investigations; 102 Congress. U.S. Government Printing Office, Washington. 1992

Suen, Andy. February 28, 1992. Deposition of 92 Productions Corp. Senate Permanent Subcommittee of Investigations Exhibit #72.

Chan, Robert (deposition transcript, Pages 1 - 51) United States Senate Permanent Subcommittee on Investigations, Committee on Governmental Affairs. Asian Organized

Bibliography

Crime. Miller Reporting Company, Inc. Washington, DC, June 9, 1992.

Quach, Calvin Thuymy (deposition transcript, Pages 1 - 87) United States Senate Permanent Subcommittee on Investigations, Committee on Governmental Affairs. Asian Organized Crime. Miller Reporting Company, Inc., Washington DC. April 9, 1992.

Black Belt Magazine. Rainbow Publications, Santa Clarita, California. April 1993 edition. Bruce Lee's Jeet Kune Do vs. Ed Parker's Kenpo Karate.

Black Belt Magazine. Rainbow Publications, Santa Clarita, California. April 1991 edition. Special Ed Parker Memorial Section.

Black Belt Magazine. Rainbow Publications, Santa Clarita, California. July 1992 edition. Bruce and Kareem! Black Belt Goes One on One with Former Hoop Star and Student of Bruce Lee!

Black Belt Magazine. Rainbow Publications, Santa Clarita, California. November 1992 edition. Chuck Norris' Anti-Drug Program.

Black Belt Magazine. Rainbow Publications, Santa Clarita, California. December 1995 edition. Black Market Bruce Lee: the Dragon's Bootleg Videotapes.
Jules Brown and Helen Lee. The Real Guide/Hong Kong and Macau. United States and Canada, Prentice Hall. 1991.

Bruce Lee: His Privacy and Anecdotes. Hong Kong, Bruce Lee JKD Society. Hui Fai, Editor. 1978.

Bruce Lee, the Untold Story. Hollywood, California. CFW Enterprises. 1979.

Cheung, Hawkins. Bruce Lee's Hong Kong Years. Inside Kung-Fu Magazine. CFW Enterprises, Inc. Burbank, California. Four parts. November 1991 – February 1992 issues.

Corcoran, John. Up Close and Personal with Stirling Silliphant. Kick Magazine. Five parts, July – November 1980 issues.

Dannen, Fredric. Hong Kong Babylon. The New Yorker, August 7, 1995.

Editors Kung-Fu Monthly. Who Killed Bruce Lee? Felden Productions, Bunch Books. 1978.

Editors Kung-Fu Monthly. Bruce Lee In Action. H. Bunch Associates, Ltd. 1977.

Inside Karate. July 1993. 20 Years After! Bruce Lee's Final Day Revisited. CFW Enterprises, Inc.

Inside Kung-Fu Magazine. CFW Enterprises, Inc. Burbank, California. December 1992 edition. IKF Exclusive! Dragon Star Jason Scott Lee!

Bibliography

Inside Kung-Fu Magazine. CFW Enterprises, Inc., Burbank, California. August 1993 edition. Linda Lee To Auction Bruce Lee Memorabilia!

Karate International. Vol.3, #2. On Film: The Life of Bruce Lee.

Karate International. Vol.3, #8. Bruce Lee: Cult of Personality.

Martial Arts Legends. Featuring Bruce Lee, the Martial Arts Wizard of Ahhhs! CFW Enterprises, Inc. January 1993.

Pan, Lynn. Lilian Likes Red (Behind the Scenes with Concubine Creator Lilian Lee). Article, Discovery (August 1992 Volume 20 Number 8). Hong Kong. Cathay Pacific Airways Ltd.

Scott, David Clark. Hong Kong's Migrant Millionaires. Article, World Monitor (Vol. 2, No. 5). The Christian Science Publishing Society. 1989.

Smoke, Stephen. Y.C. Chiang. Inside Kung-Fu Magazine. CFW Enterprises, Inc. Burbank, California. June 1976 edition.

Snyder, Joe. Official Karate Magazine. Bruce Lee's Judo Connection.

Sutton, Alan. The Kung Fu of Yun Chung Chiang... A Life's Journey. Inside Kung-Fu Magazine. CFW Enterprises, Inc.